D1447717

GH
TON

ays

on Seaside Town

an

DEVON BOOKS

CSU

First published in Great Britain in 1987 by Devon Books

ISBN: 0 86114–811–8

British Library Cataloguing in Publication Data

Norman, P.
    Budleigh Salterton in bygone days.
    1. Budleigh Salterton (Devon) ———— History
    I. Title II. Spurway, E.
    942.3'57   DA690. B8935

    ISBN: 0-86114-811-8

Printed and bound in Great Britain by A. Wheaton & Co. Ltd

DEVON BOOKS

Official Publisher to Devon County Council
An imprint of Wheaton Publishers Ltd, a member of Pergamon/BPCC Publishing Corporation PLC

Wheaton Publishers Ltd
Hennock Road, Marsh Barton, Exeter, Devon EX2 8RP
Tel: 0392 74121; Telex 42794 (WHEATN G)

SALES
Direct sales enquiries to Devon Books at the address above.
Trade sales to: Town & Country Books, P.O. Box 31, Newton Abbot,
Devon TQ12 5AQ. Tel: 080 47 2690

CONTENTS

HOW THIS BOOK
CAME ABOUT

For his annual holiday in Budleigh Salterton in the summer of 1984, Mr W.J. Gooding came to stay at Lion House. My husband and I invited him and his wife Laura for a drink. The conversation soon turned to Budleigh Salterton as it used to be, and memories just poured out of Mr Gooding. We listened in amazement and realized before long, that unless they were recorded there would soon be nobody to remember. We encouraged him to write his memories down, and I promised that I would type them – and we would see what would come of it. Mr Gooding didn't need a lot of persuasion. In fact he admitted that he had often thought of writing something like it. Autumn came, and with it the first batch of his manuscript. This continued throughout the winter. I then realized, that if it was to be published, photographs would be a valuable aid and addition. In my search for such photographs I was referred to Mrs Pat Norman who was delighted to cooperate. Over the previous few years she had been acquiring individual photos of old Budleigh Salterton, mostly picture postcards, and as her interest grew, so did her collection. It took a lot of time and a lot of effort to match the photographs and the text, but again and again we were amazed how accurate Mr Gooding's memories had been – for he had written his text without the aid of photographs, a truly remarkable feat. It was planned that he should come to Budleigh Salterton shortly after Easter 1986 to help write the captions for the photographs we had selected. It was not to be; Mr Gooding died suddenly on 11 March.

Mrs Norman and I are greaty indebted to the people who helped finish the work, checking the text and captions, and providing names and additional information. We are indebted especially to Mr Gilbert Cowd for names, accurate dates and historical details and also the odd story. Mrs Kathleen Deller, (née Gooding), helped out with information about the Bathing Station and family matters. Mrs P. Trick. (née Hitt), added valuable information about certain people and activities in the town. Mr W. Bedford kindly offered to check the text for typing and other errors. Finally, Mr Gooding's sons Jim and Ken added further details about their father's life. We are also greatly indebted to Fairlynch Museum, especially Miss Joy Gawne, for supplying us with photos we still needed to complete our record, and also to individual residents of Budleigh Salterton who allowed us to reproduce private photographs. These include the Gooding family, Mr W. Bedford, Mrs Ivy Heard, Mrs M.T. Snow, Mrs Lynda Evans, Mrs Clarke, Mrs A. Wilson, Mr Cyril Teed, Mr P.H. Curtis, Mrs Jack Wilson and Charlotte Money.

Mrs Elisabeth Spurway

Budleigh Salterton, 31 August 1986

1

ABOUT THE AUTHOR

In the text of the book, my father, Walter James Gooding (known locally as Jim), said very little about himself, and I, being his eldest son, would wish to tell you a little of his life, background and what urged him to set down his recollections of Budleigh Salterton.

He was born on 2 April 1904 in Poplar Row, which was then a row of small two-up, two-down terraced houses. Under this roof most of the family of fourteen were born and raised.

His father, to whom he refers repeatedly in the text, was a very important person for him. But that should not hide the fact that he had a very close relationship with his mother. She died when he was eighteen.

In spite of his humble origin and lack of education – like many others of his generation, he left school at an early age in order to add a few shillings to the family income – my father turned out to be far from an 'April Fool'. Through the years he read and took great interest in the world around him and acquired a great deal of knowledge and wisdom. He was particularly intrigued with people, nature and all the things that God provides for the enjoyment of those with an eye to behold.

He married my mother in 1923, and was lucky enough to rent a room in Jocelyn Road with Mr and Mrs Moxey. Mr Moxey was at that time a signalman with the South Western Railway. I have only vague recollections of this house where I was born, but it was again very cramped and lacking in facilities.

My mother and father worked hard and saved enough to buy their own house, 'Whitemoor' in Stoneborough Lane. It was a nice three-bedroomed house, built by the firm of J.W.

Palmer. The quarter-acre of garden was of course undeveloped, and in his 'spare' time, with his love of landscape gardening, my father made the garden into pleasurable as well as productive surroundings. My mother also took in visitors in the summer season to help make ends meet.

In the winter months my father would take on any labouring jobs available; the average weekly wage was only 29s. He was also in demand at Christmastime as an auxiliary postman. His knowledge of the area made him a 'regular', and it was probably this that gave him the intimate knowledge of the town which he was able to record.

During all these years he was a partner in Goodings Bros Bathing Station, which gave very good service to the town and the summer visitors. However, the outbreak of the Second World War brought an end to this: the beach was barbed-wired.

After a few years with a fish-and-chip business in Exmouth, my father and mother 'emigrated' to West Drayton, Middlesex, to carry on successfully in the same line of work for twenty-five years, until my father's retirement.

Through the prosperity of the business they eventually bought a newly built bungalow at Richings Park, Iver, Buckinghamshire which stood on nine acres of ground. My father developed this into a lovely home, and the garden and land gave him much pleasure. He named it 'Budleigh', which shows that although he lived and worked in a 'foreign' county, his heart and thoughts were still in the place of his birth.

All this time his interest in horticulture continued, and up to his death he kept a garden to be proud of. Most important, his love of the West Country and in particular Budleigh Salterton was always paramount. He visited the area as often as his business would permit, and even shorty before his death endeavoured to return to his birthplace.

We are all very proud of his efforts to record his memories of Budleigh Salterton for posterity and hope they will give you as much enjoyment to read them as they gave him to write them.

Jim Gooding Jnr

4

EARLY DAYS AT
POPLAR ROW

I was born on the second day of April 1904 at No 3 Poplar Row, the fourteenth child of Eli and Emily Gooding. My family used to tease me by saying I was hidden under the bed for a few hours so that I could be registered on 2 April to avoid being an 'April Fool', which would have caused me a lot of embarrassment as I grew up.

The house, or cottage it might be called, had the usual appearance of a working-class home at that time. One entered by two steps direct into the living-room, which was also the kitchen, with the usual cooking stove, with oven, the only means of cooking being with coal. There was no gas or electricity in dwellings of that sort in those days, and all water had to be heated on the stove. To get the first cup of tea in the morning, you had to light the fire to boil the kettle, and if the sticks had not been dried overnight, it would be a lengthy and tiresome job.

The stove was flanked by two cupboards, one on either side, which to my recollection were the only means of storing food, etc. The walls were constructed of cob, subsoil of the area mixed with straw to bind it together – mixed much as concrete would be today – and encased in shuttering (wooden boards) until set. The windows were the casement type, set back in the wall. The thickness of the wall afforded room for a window seat for two, which meant more space around the room and two less chairs.

Off this room, opposite the door, was a room always known as the parlour, although it was never used as such. There was a bed in there, which was kept in case of sickness, or, as was often the case, for one of the older girls of the family, should they be at home for some reason. For it was customary for the girls of school-leaving age to go into service at one of the bigger houses of the town owned by those generally known as 'the gentry'.

To the right of the parlour was a passage leading to what would later be known as the 'backhouse', or scullery, which I remember had a very low sink, about six inches deep, but no tap. This was just outside the door and a constant source of trouble in winter because of freezing. Then an outside toilet, which was 'on the mains', but had no flushing cistern. You had to pour a bucket of water down to flush it. Beyond this, further down the yard, were three cells, used by the police for detaining people overnight, usually vagrants or beggars, of which there were many in those days. The house used to be occupied by a policeman, before what is known now as 'The Old Clink' became the police station of the day. Also in the yard was the usual shed or linhay, which was used for storage purposes.

The stairs, at the end of the passage on the right, leading to the two bedrooms, were a narrow and rickety affair which used to creak at every step. There was no landing as such, just a wider step at the top. Straight ahead was the

The complete Gooding family, but not in correct order of age. When the original photograph was taken the younger children had not been born. Their photographs were superimposed into the picture at a later date. The author, the youngest of the fourteen children is the small boy in the check dress on the extreme left.

bedroom which contained my parents' bed and a very large cot which the youngest child slept in until either old enough to sleep away from the parents, or grew too big to sleep there comfortably. There was little else in the room. I remember the dressing table consisted of two tin trunks, draped over with some sort of material and topped with a small swing-mirror.

The second bedroom had a sloping ceiling, which was about three feet high at its lowest point, and one double bed longways in the room. This used to sleep three or four boys, according to how many were home at the time. The unfortunate one sleeping on the inside of the bed had to be very careful not to bash his head on the low ceiling. The other bed, a smaller, four-foot one, slept two of the younger ones, who graduated to the larger bed as they grew older.

Poplar Row, looking east towards Fairlynch, now the local museum

The sleeping accommodation for the girls was, until they left home for service, the bed in the parlour, or a small bed in the main bedroom.

If I have taken a lot of space in describing the house, it is that I have tried to tell you of the general conditions of that time. Of course, all families were not as large as ours, but usually had between five and eight children.

I shall now try to describe our neighbours, who would be very much like the working-classes of the period. Poplar Row was unusual in that it had houses on only one side. In No 1 was a widow woman called Pengilley; she had one son called Walter, who was only at home at infrequent periods. The old lady gave me a small toy lamb which I still possess, much battered now as it was a plaything in turn of my own three children. It must be at least 100 years old; Walter was a grown man when first I knew him, and it was his toy in his childhood.

In No 2 was a family called Davie which consisted, if I remember rightly, of six or seven. No 4 had an old lady whose name I never did know correctly. I think it was Leash, but was

Mrs Gooding in Poplar Row, with neighbour Mrs Pengilley

7

always pronounced 'Lass'. She was a washerwoman, a widow of many years. We boys always had the job of collecting the washing on the Monday and delivering it to the big houses early on Fridays. And we always had to give the old lady a hand turning the mangle, a huge contraption with two wooden rollers through which the wet laundry was passed by turning the big wheel which in turn, by means of cog-wheels, turned the rollers and squeezed the water out after rinsing by hand. The laundry was then hung out on clotheslines to dry, a difficult job in wet weather. And remember, it had to be returned by Friday. Sometimes wet laundry would be spread on the beach where it dried quickly on the warm pebbles. But I don't remember our neighbour doing so.

There was a wide passage between this and the next three houses. It led to a small builder's yard which was used by Mr Cowd who lived in the end house against Pebble Lane. He built several houses and was known as 'Little Fred', to distinguish him from 'Big Fred' Cowd who lived in another part of the town. No 5 had as a tenant for many years another widow, called Emmett, a very devout woman who used to like one of us children to have tea with her on Sunday evening. In fact we used to take our own tea. She would make a pot of tea – she could not afford anything else – and after tea she would always read from the Bible, or get us to do so when we were old enough to read. Poverty was rife in those days, and when Mr Lloyd George's pension scheme came in, around 1908, it was only five shillings a week. Heaven only knows how people used to manage before that. We did not consider ourselves poor, but I remember being sent first thing in the morning to Daniels, the haberdashers', with a small piece of lace that my mother had worked on till late at night, burning the midnight oil, and I would be given a shilling, with which I went to the baker's to buy bread for our breakfast. People helped each other then, and when the fishing was poor during the winter months, the shopkeepers, whether baker, butcher or grocer, would supply food to families on credit. With the first good catches of fish the debts would be repaid, and the fishermen and families only felt happy again when all debts were paid off.

Many women did lacemaking at home to help feed their families. My grandmother Slade, from an Old Sidmouth family, is reputed to have been one of the ladies of that town whose lace was used to make up a christening gown for the royal family, and, we are told, it is still being used.

No 6 Poplar Row housed Mr and Mrs Bucknell, two very old people, or so they seemed to us children. At the Pebble Lane end of the Row was a green door leading to a garden and small orchard. Down Pebble Lane were two cottages which we thought of as part of Poplar Row. They were demolished to make way for the garages of the present houses in Poplar Row, as by this time the motor car was becoming part of the way of life.

My father, whose family came from Colaton Raleigh, was born at East Budleigh, and was a farm worker before coming to Budleigh Salterton, supposedly to earn a bigger wage than the agricultural wage of the times. I have heard him say that when he left school at the age of ten he went to work at the same farm as his father, Tidwell Farm, and their combined wages were twelve shillings a week. He could neither read nor write but could, as he put it, 'read figures'. You could give him the longest sum imaginable and he would give you the answer before I could have reckoned it on paper. But he could not write it down. Schooling was not compulsory, and a scholar attending the village school was charged 1d. a week, which I think may have been the reason for his leaving school so early. His father must have found it very hard to find the money.

From my earliest recollections he was a fisherman, and always had to work very hard indeed to feed and clothe so large a family. He was a very big man, weighing sixteen stones in his prime, with not an ounce of fat on him. It must have run in the family, for I was told that his mother, Caroline Gooding, was also a very big woman, and when Eli on her death in 1910, took her wedding ring from her hand, he had to have it made smaller so that he could wear it.

One of the things I remember about my father is how, when the herrings were carried up the beach to be put into barrels waiting on the wall, two men would carry roughly two hundred fish between them in a two-handled basket called a 'maund'. But he would carry a barrel of four hundred fish, if it was lifted up to his shoulder, and put it on the wall unaided. This was no

Eli Gooding and 'Trooper' Sedgemore

unusual feat, as in those days flour was packed into 240lb sacks and men would be expected to carry them to and from the delivery wagons. Men used to boast and tell stories of their achievements and I remember him saying on one occasion, when being told a rather tall story, 'I wouldn't believe it if I knew it was true', and left the teller of the story to work out for himself what he meant. In his later days he used to go to the Bathing Station, in which he still had a financial interest, and visitors and residents alike would talk to him to hear his opinion about the weather and anything topical in the town at the time. Often he would not be easily understood as he always spoke in the Devonshire dialect, and coming from East Budleigh it was much broader than usual, as was the case in all the villages inland. To illustrate my point, a feature of the summer weather was the wind following the sun around, and when light breezes were the pattern, there was a smooth sea all the time. Sometimes, however, then as now, the wind would freshen and the sea would get very rough, but the wind would quickly come around to the north-west, and the sea would be calm in a short time. On one such occasion a

gentleman visitor said to him, 'Well, Gooding, what do you think of the weather?' My father took a knowing glance at the sky and in his rich Devon accent said, 'Aw, 'e'll be off um bye, zur'. Seeing the gentleman's puzzled look he explained that he thought the wind would veer to the north-west and that it would be a fine evening. The gentleman then said, 'Oh, I see'; but I doubt if he really did. He then said, 'So you refer to the wind as in terms of 'he'. Now about this 'um bye' you mention. What does this imply?' My father then explained that it meant some time later in the day, and I have often heard it said in conversation. In correct English it was, of course, 'bye and bye'.

On another occasion a visitor who had been to Budleigh Salterton often and knew my father well said to him, 'How many children have you had, Gooding?', and he replied, 'Fourteen zur, and twelve of 'em living'. 'My word', was the reply, 'now you are getting older, you won't have to work, with all those children'. My father looked at him long and earnestly and asked whether he had ever seen young birds feeding the old ones.

Another incident I remember illustrated what a big powerful man he was. As a young man I was working in a garden across the railway line by what was then a wooden foot-bridge (now replaced by an iron structure), a long way from the beach. It was a lovely autumn afternoon and I distinctly heard my father selling fish. He used to buy local catches and hawk them in the street, shouting his wares as he went along. When I saw him in the evening I asked him who had caught the whiting. He replied, 'How did you know that there was any whiting caught?', knowing what part of the town I had been working in. I said that I had heard him selling them, and he then told me he nad not started selling until he reached Fore Street and had finished when he reached the junction of High Street and Station Road. If he had been able to read, he would have made a wonderful town crier.

In those days almost everyone in the town seemed to have a nickname, used not only in the family, but also when talking to or about other people. Our family nickname was 'Rummager', and I have often heard people call my father by his nickname, although we, as children, were forbidden to refer to any adult by their nickname and were punished if we were caught doing so.

Other children, as well as grown-ups, would always call us by this name, and it was taken for granted. In our family, my eldest brother was called 'Hooting Sillo', Fred was 'Striker', Frank was 'Mumbler', Herman was 'Badger', Arthur was 'Lobot', and I was always 'Biggie'. I can't remember my three oldest sisters being called by nicknames, probably because they were in service and therefore not at home much in my early youth. But I do remember my sister Bessie was 'Guss' or 'Gussie'. Elsie was 'Taster', and Violet was 'Gargle'. In most cases there was a definite reason for the nickname; Violet, for example, suffered from sore throats and tonsillitis and often had to gargle to get relief. If there were two generations of a family living they would be referred to as 'Old Harry' and 'Young Harry'. For instance, there was Old Harry Rogers and Young Harry Rogers, Old George Pearcey and Young George Pearcey. Young Harry Rogers always referred to his sons by their nickname, 'Digger' and 'Father Lion'.

But I must move on, as my family moved on from Poplar Row to 18 High Street, to 33 Fore Street and 19 Fore Street, and finally to The Glen.

THE BEACH

When I refer to 'the beach' I mean the whole beach, starting from the River Otter's mouth to Straight Point, a stretch of about three miles, and not just the section in front of the town, or the only part to interest the casual visitor.

To any observant person who is interested enough to make the walk, now and again, to the mouth of the river, it will become clear that sometimes the Otter flows on the east side of the ledge of the rocks that are known to local fishermen as Island Rocks; but after a series of easterly winds that channel becomes blocked by pebbles, which enables the adventurous to walk dry-footed on to the rocks. It was, and still is, a way of spending an interesting time among the pools, where a varied selection of shellfish and other things such as small crabs and fish will be found. But great care should be taken not to get

The Bay and the beach looking westward from Saltings Hill to Straight Point

River Mouth with Island Rocks looking eastwards from Saltings Hill

A group of boats on the landward side of Pebble Ridge, on the River Otter

South Bridge before it was washed away by floodwater

cut off by a rising tide, and no one should undertake this adventure once the tide has started coming in.

There used to be a path right to the river mouth. It turned round in a loop at the end, and this turn was known to locals as 'Donkey's Turn', for you could drive along it with a donkey and cart or even a horse and wagon. That path, alas, is no more: it was swept away, if I remember rightly, in a storm in the early part of 1970. Now you have to walk on rough pebbles to get to the river mouth. Just there, if you face the sea, there was, and still is, on the right a very shallow beach, known as 'The Catch'. It is different from the rest of the bay in that it is shallow water, and I can remember large catches of bass and grey mullet being caught at this spot in the early days of my youth. If you faced inland, a very fine view of the river estuary could be seen, as far as South Bridge.

At one time there were two pools in the river, known as Higher and Lower Salmon Pools, where the local fishermen used to poach for salmon, which was illegal. As was often the case, the fishermen were very religious people, and they oftentimes made the excuse that God meant the salmon for all and not just for the chosen few. Right against the river mouth on the seaward side there was a small group of fishing boats and a capstan, known now as a winch, owned by a fisherman called Jimmy Ford. He was a devout Christian and, like my father and others, would never fish on Sundays, and would only go to sea on Saturdays on condition that the boat was ashore by midnight. On the land side of the path, opposite this collection of boats, was another lot of boats owned by various people who used the river as far as tidal waters would allow, some for pleasure and others for the limited fishing that was available.

There was also a boat owned by the council and used by the man who operated the opening and closing of the new sewer. Almost every road in the town had been opened to lay the new pipes, and this operation was continued along the Parade until it reached the old lime-kiln, where the pipe was connected to a tunnel extending to the cliffs on the other side of the River Otter. There was a shaft at the lime-kiln end, 18 feet deep, and at the other end a shaft 180 feet deep. At the top of this shaft was a hut which contained the winding-gear which opened and closed the outlet at the foot of

Banoss Mears operating a capstan

Steamer landing at Steamer Steps. The *Duke* and *Duchess* made regular trips from Lyme Regis to Torquay and back, calling in at the towns along the coast

the cliffs below. The outlet had to be opened twice a day at high tide, and closed again about an hour after the tide had turned to come in, so that the tunnel would empty when the tide receded. The opening and closing was done manually, which is why the council kept a boat on the beach to enable the man to cross the river. But at times, as when the river was in flood, it would be highly dangerous to do so. So the poor man had no alternative but to make the trip, day or night, up the banks of the river to South Bridge and back on the other bank to the hut. I expect there is now some mechanical means of doing this operation.

But back to the beach. The section between the shaft and the lime-kiln was known as 'The Bight'. It was often used during strong easterly winds, as the ledge of the rocks afforded sheltered landings. At the point referred to by local fishermen as the 'Lime-Kiln', was another group of boats, much larger than the one near the river mouth, and another capstan, also owned by Jimmy Ford. He lived in a small cottage in a lane beyond the beach, about half a mile away, and kept a seine-boat on this part of the beach.

Continuing westward toward the town we come to the main part of the beach, used for bathing and fishing. It ends at the Steamer Steps, still called by that name long after the passenger steamers had ceased to call there. Steamer trips used to be a very popular form of entertainment, and no wonder; very few people had a motor car. The *Duke* and *Duchess of Devonshire*, stationed at Exmouth and Torquay called at Salterton for as long as I can remember; the *Duke* was sold in 1932, and the *Duchess* was wrecked two years later on the beach at Sidmouth, There was also a pleasure steamer called the *Alexandra*, which used to come from Weymouth and went on to Torquay. It operated from 1925 to 1928, but I don't know its final fate.

The section between the lime-kiln and the foot of Coastguard Hill was mainly used for bathing, and after the First World War, the beach became fashionable for deck chairs and the provision of refreshments. The part of the beach near the foot of Coastguard Hill was referred to as 'The Bathing Machines'; although why they were called 'machines' has always remained , to me at any rate, a mystery.

The next section extended from the Bathing Machines to the proximity of the East Devon Club House, known by the locals as the Gentlemen's Club. This point was Pole Head, in local pronunciation 'Pool Aid', and the stretch in between was known as The Parade. This part of the beach was kept clear of any form of obstruction, except for a larger collection of boats and capstans, more or less for the use of the fishermen, who occupied the site long before any houses were built on The Parade. Every fishing family used to have its own section of beach into which no other family intruded. The Parade was separated from the roadway by a wall and iron railings, and seats were provided on the promenade for people's enjoyment.

Beyond Pole Head westward to the Steamer Steps was known as 'Back of the Cliff'. It had the largest collection of fishing boats and capstans and included the bigger boats, the drifters or crabbers which were up to 25 feet long. Here were also, at different points along the beach, many small boats, about 10 to 12 feet long. These were used for pleasure, and hired out to residents and visitors, at a fee that now seems very cheap indeed.

Westward from the Steamer Steps the beach narrows, and is backed by red sandstone cliffs studded with pebbles and rising to a height of 500 feet. At intervals along these cliffs, which end at Straight Point, are various points used as landmarks by fishermen to locate fishing-grounds. I do not remember them all, but one, not far from the Steamer Steps, was called the 'Pulpit'. It was a cleft in the lower section of the cliff, which I suppose gave it the name, roughly under the spot known then as 'Mackerel Square' (in local pronunciation 'Mackel Square'). The name Mackerel Square has now been moved to the area at the end of Fore Street at the junction of Fore Street Hill, near the Old Clink and opposite The Glen. But it is a misnaming of the area, which in my time was known as The Square.

West from the Pulpit was Hackley, with Hackley Field on top of the cliff, once a cultivated area that, together with the grounds that came to be named Jubilee Plantation, was given to Salterton as a public recreation ground by Lord Mark Rolle on the occasion of Queen Victoria's Diamond Jubilee in 1897. Access from the Cliff Walk was through an elaborate wicket gate. Onward to Sherbrook Chine, which at one time you could descend by a winding path to the beach.

Looking east from Mackerel Square

Then westward to West Down Beacon, the highest part of the cliffs, also called 'The Flagstaff' because there was a coastguard hut and a flagstaff at this point. Then come The Floors, where the cliffs become less steep and were, in my early days, the home for quite a number of foxes. Further west was The Cove, a good spot for early catches of mackerel. Then on to Straight Point, by which time the cliffs are much lower.

On top of the cliffs runs the cliff path, with several changes in direction because sections of the cliff fell away in the course of time. The erosion is usually a gradual process, and the path has to be set back from the cliff edge accordingly. Early this century the cliff path, which now zigzags back and forth, led up in a straight run past the Rosemullion Hotel (then on the south side of Hackley Field), and on reaching a gate turned left, then right, following the hedge around the field. This portion was called 'The Quarter Deck', using naval language, and because it afforded a marvellous view over Torbay, several seats were provided. This section of the cliff path has now disappeared owing to various cliff falls,

The wicket gate giving access to Jubilee Plantation

Sherbrook Chine. It was mined during the
Second World War. One of the mines was set off
accidentally by three soldiers making their way
to the beach

West Down Beacon beyond the Chine

The Floors with a hunting party

referred to by locals as 'rusers'. There have also been cliff falls further west, one of the largest occurring near The Flagstaff in 1920. The most tragic one happened near the town below the present shelter, shortly before Christmas 1901. Some little boys were playing in a shallow cave when suddenly the front of the cliff slid down and buried them. The funeral was on Christmas Eve, and it was the saddest Christmas the town has ever known.

The formation of the beach is very different now, although it is gradually regaining its old character. It was at one time, I believe, the second largest pebble beach in England, second only to Chesil Beach at Portland. It was then, as now, formed by ridges of pebbles known locally as 'cops'. As you walked along the seafront you could not see the high- or low-water marks, as the main pebble ridge or cop was some 6 or 8 feet above the path. This ridge was formed by extreme westerly gales during the turn of the century and remained intact until the late forties, when a series of gales removed it and most of the remaining pebbles, with the result that the 'big cop' was lowered to about 8 feet *below* the path. It caused a lot of anxiety about the safety of The Parade westward from the Bathing Station and the path eastward under the cliffs.

Beyond the lime-kiln where there is now an extensive car park, were the tidal marshes, and in olden times, salt-pans. The making of salt was carried out under the supervision of monks from Otterton Priory, a small outpost of the monastery of St Michael's Mount. From this industry the town got the second part of its name. Budleigh is an offshoot of East Budleigh, which was in existence long before there was a settlement on the coast.

The cliff path early this century ran up in a straight line to Hackley Field. However, as a result of cliff falls it has almost completely disappeared. The semi-circular widening of the path just below the top of the cliffs was called the 'The Pulpit'

Tidal marshes and salt-pans. Notice the path on the ridge of pebbles with 'Donkey's Turn' at the end

FISHING

Herring-drifting was one of the main industries of the town during my early years and while it lasted, gave Budleigh Salterton a certain importance. There were about a dozen drifters, ranging from 18 to 25 feet in length. They carried anything from twelve to twenty nets according to the quantity of fish expected, which on reaching the fishing-ground, were shot out in a straight run, secured to the mast and then allowed to drift with the tide. They formed a wall of net suspended by cork floats at the depth required. The head-lines of the nets had corks every 2 yards or so, to keep the net upright in the water. The larger boats carried a crew of three, the smaller ones, two. When in luck, the nets were full of herrings, which actually caught themselves by swimming into the nets. This type of fishing was always carried out in the hours of darkness. On landing the fish, the boats with their catch, were hauled up the beach above the high-water mark, and anyone who had helped was given a

Herring Drifters

A good catch of herrings. The author is one of the small lads

number of fish for their family consumption. In the morning there was great activity, and according to the number of fish caught – up to 40 000 a boat – extra help would be needed to unload the catch and carry the fish to the cliff path. Here the buyer's agent packed them into barrels holding seven or eight hundred fish, covered the top of the barrel with hessian and secured it with a steel hoop hammered over the top. The barrels were then labelled, taken by horse-drawn transport to the railway station, and dispatched to various parts of the country, including Exeter, Plymouth and London. The boats were cleaned down, the nets restored and made ready for the next trip.

Each boat was fitted with one or more oil-filled hurricane lanterns, one of which would be hauled to the mast-head as darkness fell. The only other equipment was a coal-fired stove, called a 'bogey' which stood on a metal tray and was sometimes used to cook herrings for a meal. The fish would be roughly scaled and gutted, and fried over the stove. I'm sure they must have been lovely and could not have been fresher, but as I was only once taken on one ot these trips, I did not experience such a delight.

In my early days there were no motor boats, and it was a grand sight to see our little fleet of drifters setting sail for the fishing-grounds and being joined by up to a hundred others, from Exmouth, Lympstone, Topsham, Sidmouth, Beer and Seaton and often by the bigger boats from Plymouth, West Bay and other places. After dark it was a pretty sight to see all the lights from the drifters – it was like another town out there, and the Berry Head lighthouse, flashing every three and thirteen seconds, completed the picture.

That scene continued with little change, except that most of the boats switched from sail to motor, until, for no apparent reason, the herring gradually ceased to visit the area. My own opinion

Packing the herrings into barrels

is that the herring came to spawn on the rough coral sea bottom, which was ideal for their purpose as it afforded an anchorage for the spawn. But as dredging for scallops became a regular thing, the coral gradually disappeared. The herring would come in plenty, as usual, but move on to find a more suitable spawning-ground. Big catches would be made for a night or so, but then it was over for the season.

During the First World War the prices realized for the catch were unrealistically high, as much as 25s. for a hundred fish. A batch of 100 was actually 120, for the fish were counted in this way: four men would pick up a fish each and put them into the basket or 'aunot', counting them as one; the men would call out the numbers in turn until the number thirty was reached, when the last man would call out 'tally'. The government later controlled all the prices, and set the retail price of herring at 8d. a pound, which put an end to high prices. At one time the price fell so low,

due to prolific catches, that the fish were sold for 1s.3d. a thousand, and the fishermen sometimes shovelled them back into the sea.

During the herring season bad weather would often spring up after the boats had gone to sea. If the wind was easterly, the Beer boats would run for shelter on our beach rather than try to get home around the treacherous Beer Head, and the crews would always be accommodated in the homes of the local fishermen for the night, small as their cottages were. What the wives of our fishermen thought about it was never talked about, as, who knows, their husbands might be glad of shelter sometime.

Another major occupation during the months from February to October was crabbing. It was known as 'onshore' and 'offshore' crabbing. The onshore grounds were not more than 1 mile out, while the offshore grounds could be up to 10 or 12 miles out. Onshore was mainly east of the ledge known as 'Up-behind' extending as far as Ladram

Harry Rogers and George Pearcey making crab pots

Baiting the crab pots. (From left to right; Banoss Mears, George Pearcey, and Harry and Will Rogers)

Bay, and also on smaller patches of rock off our own bay, the main one being known as 'Footclout'. You may wonder how the fishermen could find the spot where the rocks were. It was done by 'staking' or aligning two marks on the shore; for example Footclout could be found by getting Shortwood over the Rolle Hotel, and the flagstaff at the Coastguard Station lined up between the second and third chimneys of the Coastguard Cottages.

Onshore boats were 12 to 14 feet long and normally had a crew of one, but sometimes two. They would fish about forty pots. They would leave shore soon after daylight, the pots being hauled in by hand, as there was no winches in those days. This was even harder work in the offshore grounds, which were in much deeper waters. Offshore comprised three main areas: the first, 'Out in the bay' was about 2 miles or so from the land; the second, 'Middle Ground' was 4 or 5 miles out; the third, known as 'The Exeters', was much further out, and only the bigger boats went that far. Two men handled the offshore boats. The pots could only be fished at certain stages of the tide, because when the tide was running at its strongest, the cork floats marking the pots would be hardly visible. This was very hard work because with no motors, the boats had to be handled with oars, or 'paddles', as they were referred to. When there was no wind, the men would 'out paddles' and row to the fishing-grounds and back. In later years, in the days of motor boats, and winches to haul in the pots, life became much easier. But until then, ideal weather would be an offshore wind going around with the sun, which gave fair winds out and back.

The catches of shellfish were sometimes sold locally by the fishermen themselves, but most were bought by Mr Redway, who had a store in Queen Street at the back of the shops. He also took a lot of mackerel and herring, and used his store to hold the boxes and barrels to pack them. This part of the trade was later done by Mr Harry Hooker, a local fish merchant, and his two sons, and also by Mr Picketts of Exmouth, known as 'Banty' Picketts.

The fishermen did not always take kindly to visitors seeking to speak to them, and when one of them was asked on one occasion 'Where did you catch these crabs?' the reply was curt, 'Up Shortwood' – Shortwood being the hill north-west of the town!

The other summertime industry was mackerel seining. There was about a dozen seining boats operating at various times. Seining could not be done satisfactorily with less than four men, and sometimes, if the catch was big enough, it would take many more. But as long as there were three to start, plenty of help was soon forthcoming. The seine-net varied in length from 200 to 300 yards, and comprised two arms, and the part between known as the 'bunt', was marked by a large cork buoy. The head-lines were fitted with cork floats, and the foot-lines with lead weights, to form a wall of net. The ends were attached to a polestaff about 4 feet long, and these served to keep the net upright in the water. A length of rope was attached to each end, and the crew would wait patiently until fish were sighted on the

Mackerel seining. Taking out the boat, and pulling in the net

23

The harvest of the sea. Tom and 'Curly' Sedgemoor

Pleasure boats for hire. They were painted in red, white and blue

surface. This was known as 'playing'; in fact it was the mackerel feeding on whitebait, or 'britt' (its local name). The rope was then thrown ashore, and the seine was thrown out in a semi-circle and hauled in to the shore, keeping the buoy marking the bunt in the centre. This was important as this part of the net was stronger. I have helped to land as many as 5000 fish in one catch.

Another form of fishing was to moor nets, known as 'trammels', overnight and haul them in early the next day. Usually plaice and other flat fish were caught by this method. And again, a long line of baited hooks was moored on the rocky bottom with a weight at each end, and a mast buoy attached. This was a method of catching various types of fish other than flat fish. This part of Budleigh Salterton's history is now over and very little fishing is carried on these days.

The fishermen had yet another occupation; hiring out small rowing boats for pleasure. This business was carried on at Pole Head, mainly by two brothers called Ambrose and Herbie Mears. Great pride was taken in the upkeep of these boats, especially by Herbie, who had four or five, painted in red, white and blue. The charge in those days was 2s. an hour without a boatman, and 2s. 6d. with. Fishing-tackle was supplied at an extra charge, and it was the custom for the boatman to take one-third of any fish caught. At Back of the Cliff, George Pearcey and Tom and Russell Sedgemore would also hire out small boats if the occasion warranted it.

The chief fishing families were the Mears, Rogers, Sedgemores and Pearceys, and in most cases consisted of the entire family, from grandfather to grandsons. There were also individual fishermen (Hitt, Pengilley, Hillman), and part-time fishermen who would carry out their usual work by day, and come to the beach during non-working hours, either fishing on their own or helping the regular fishermen. There was Harry Pratt, a painter, George Underhill, a master baker, and Red Wilson who was a chauffeur-gardener to Dr Semple – and by the way, drove the first car in Budleigh Salterton. There were others no less important, whose names I have forgotten. These part-timers always worked with the same professional fishermen and would not dream of helping another crew unless asked to do so.

There were also one or two amateur fishermen. One was called Bill Cowd, who, with his father, worked as a carpenter for Palmers the builders. He lived in a house in South Parade by the quay wall. When Bill junior was quite young, his father built him a flat-bottomed boat, half boat, half canoe. From then on, young Bill was hooked on the beach and fishing. In later years, he owned a small motor boat and used to fish on fine evenings towing a small 'Otter' trawl. He was never happier than when on the beach or at sea, and was always accepted by the professionals who would gladly give him any advice or help if he needed it.

A notable landmark in the fishing industry was the arrival of the first motor boat. The engine was installed in a former sailing drifter, the *Victory*. It was known as a 'Belfast Barker' and lived up to its name; it could not have had a silencer attached as it could be heard approaching from miles away. It was not very reliable and was always causing trouble, which used to infuriate the owner, Mr Sedgemore, nicknamed 'Curly'. He was so disgusted with it on one occasion that he offered to sell it for nothing – an offer, if it had been taken up I very much doubt he would have accepted. Of course in later years, marine engines were much improved, were very reliable, and seldom, if ever, caused their owners any trouble. But the early problems were never forgotten, and there was always a pair of oars included in the equipment, in case of a breakdown. And there was always an anchor, or slingstone if having to moor on a rocky bottom (a slingstone was used, as an anchor would be more likely to get caught in the rock and have to be cut away).

Bill Sedgemore and his wife Jemima must have been one of the most colourful couples in Budleigh Salterton and I could write pages about their doings. Bill was always to be seen on the beach or around Back of the Cliff. On one occasion, he found himself there along with a number of local fishermen and others who mainly through age or infirmity were not working. The time would be about noon on a lovely spring day. They were seated in the shelter under the cliff path by what was then the Rolle Hotel. They were almost drowsy, enjoying the early spring sunshine, for the sun, being low in the sky at that time of the year, was shining right into the shelter. All was quiet, every topic of conversation having long been exhausted. The silence was broken by a wealthy American visitor who, as it was a lovely day, wanted to hire a boat and a boatman to take him and his two young daughters fishing, and would have been willing to pay well. The first enquiry met with complete silence, possibly because the men were asleep, but, more likely because nobody wanted to break their lovely siesta. (It must be said in defence of the fishermen, that the boats that would have been suitable for the occasion had been hauled to the top of the beach, and it would have taken several men half an hour or longer to get one ready and launched.) The next enquiry was said more loudly, and with a feeling that it could not be ignored, William Sedgemore, as usual the spokesman of the party said, 'Wull, zur, tiz like this yer, I doubt if thur's other veesh alive within a 'underd mile of this yer place' (Well, sir, it's like this here, I very much doubt it we should find any fish within 100 miles of here), and promptly returned to enjoy his nap in the sun.

A WALK ABOUT
THE TOWN

On the way to East Budleigh the town more or less finished at the Cottage Hospital, except for a few buildings here and there. And again, going towards Exmouth, it was the same at Links Road. We will start our walk around the town at the Cottage Hospital. That this hospital ever came about was largely due to the Revd J.B. Boucher, who contributed very generously towards its building in 1887 – to commemorate the Golden Jubilee of Queen Victoria – and equally generously endowed it. The ground was given by the Hon. Mark Rolle. The original building had only a dozen or so beds, but the hospital was later enlarged at various stages, with the help of public subscriptions. Today's Health Service may not be perfect, but it is far superior to the old system. In my younger days, if you were poor, only the husband would be admitted to hospital, and only if he could obtain a 'recommend' from one of the influential people of the town, who would then pay for him. A later scheme covered hospital stays for all the family, for a payment of about 2d. a week.

If we bear left off East Budleigh Road we come into Coastguard Road. The triangle of land enclosed by East Budleigh Road, Coastguard Road and Granary Lane was, with the exception of Stoneborough House and a few cottages belonging to it, all agricultural land. Stoneborough House, situated a fair way out along East Budleigh Road, was quite an estate, with cottages and houses for craftsmen and other staff

employed in the house and on the land. It was famed for the annual ball, given on New Year's Eve or thereabouts, for the sons and daughters of the local tradesmen and farmers. The house was pulled down in 1960 to give way to 'progress', and where Stoneborough House once stood there is now a block of flats called by the same name.

All the houses on the north side of Coastguard Road have been built since the First World War with the exception of the Old Vicarage, now converted to flats. Originally the house was called Addiston, and was owned by Lady Alice Ewing who gave it to the parish together with Glebe Cottage next door, which was the groom's home. The other houses were built in Webber's Field, which was formerly used by visiting fairs, including the famous Anderton and Rowlands'. On the seaward side of the road the large houses have gone. Only Fernie Knowe, an apartment house in my time, is still left. Otterbourne House next to it, owned by Lady Mathieson, was turned into a hotel between the wars, and later demolished and rebuilt as flats. Cintra, next door, took the name of the original house, presumably because the owner of the older Cintra moved to this new, much smaller house. The original Cintra was a very imposing residence. Its name was later changed to White Lodge, and this was retained for the present block of flats which replaces the old house. Its garden used to go right down to the road over Coastguard Hill, as

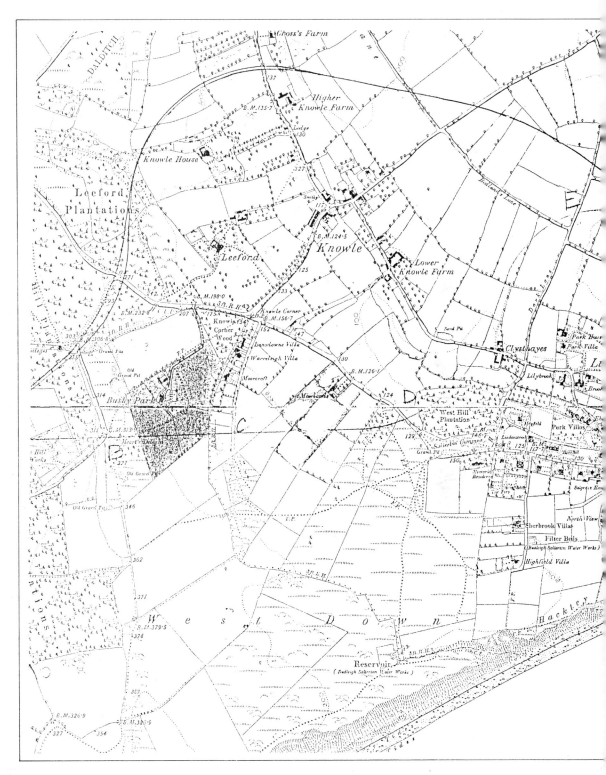

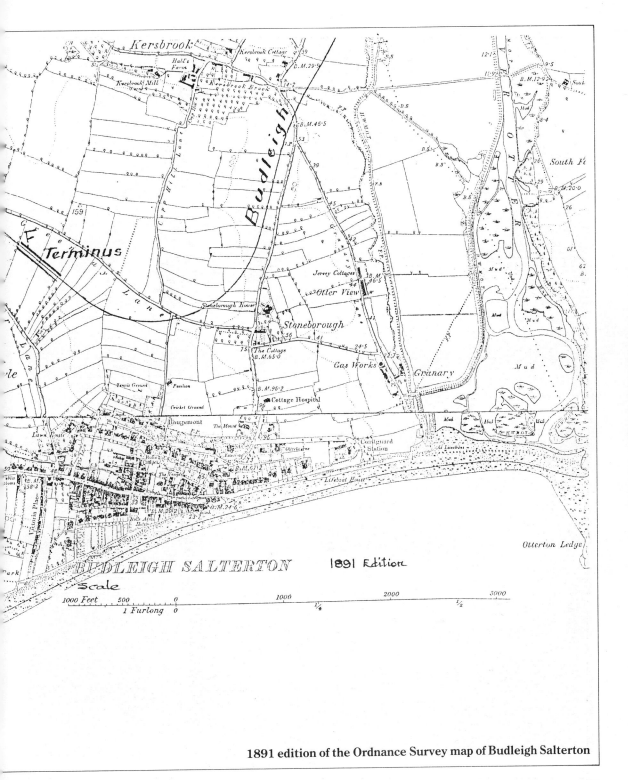

1891 edition of the Ordnance Survey map of Budleigh Salterton

Aerial view of Budleigh Salterton. It shows Coastguard Road with Otterbourne House, Cintra, the Coastguard Cottages, Ottermouth House, Coastguard Hill and the original Eastcliff House and Marine Parade

Otterbourne House

did the gardens of The Chance next door. It was at Cintra that I had my first job, cleaning boots and knives. I had to be at the house by 7 a.m., work until 8 a.m., and after having been given breakfast, I went on to school. After school, at around 4.30 p.m., I used to go back to clean any shoes or knives that had been used, and to take letters to the post. For this, a six-day week, I received 2s.6d. When I was a little older, I used to work all day Saturday doing various jobs in and around the house and garden, and during school holidays, I worked there all week. One of the first things I had to do was to caddy for the gentleman of the house, Mr Hughes, and I remember how proud I was when he took me through the town to the golf links in his motor car. I think I must have been the first boy in Budleigh Salterton to ride in a motor car. Mr Hughes had taken a liking to me, I can't think why. He told my parents he would like to have me, on leaving school, as a valet and I have often wondered since what difference it would have made to my life. Fancy me, a gentleman's gentleman! Sadly Mr Hughes died before it could come to pass.

The Coastguard Cottages further along the road were built in 1885 for the Admiralty for the use of the members of the Coastguard who manned the Watch House twenty-four hours a day. The main duties were watching for vessels in distress and keeping a look-out for smuggling, which in earlier days was a very active trade on this part of the coast. There was a tall flag-pole with a yard-arm on the lawn between the cottages and the Watch House. The white ensign was hoisted at sunrise and lowered at sunset, a ceremony which could be seen from various vantage points in the town. I am told that the white ensign was donated by Mr Trick, grandson of the Coastguard Officer, to the Fairlynch Museum, where it is now on show. The cottages have very small windows – small enough to prevent any escape if the Petty Officer of the Watch called and the coastguard for some reason, did not want to see him – that was the belief of the local people at that time. I suppose the cottages were considered good accommodation for the rank and file of the service in those times. They had no inside tap or sink, the toilet was at the end of the garden, and there was one communal wash-house for the eight houses and one for the two houses allocated to the Petty Officers.

On the other side of Coastguard Road as it turns around the bend there was originally a large house called Ottermouth built for Mr Ellis, an Exeter jeweller, and his wife. It was later taken over and run as a hotel by two American ladies, and then had at least three further owners before it was pulled down and replaced by several blocks of flats, now known as Blueberry Downs. The boundary wall that runs from the war memorial at the end of Coastguard Road down the hill towards the Otter mouth is constructed, as you cannot fail to notice, of large pebbles from the beach and topped with natural rocks from the east side of the river mouth.

Down the hill we come to what is left of the old lime-kilns, which used to supply farmers and other people with lime. They were almost

Ottermouth House in the snow (later replaced by Blueberry Downs)

Pencil sketch of the old lime-kilns (1837)

completely destroyed to make way for a one-way system to the car park. Lime-burning was an old local industry, and limestone was brought in by ships, landed at high tide as close as possible to the shore, and at low tide run up in trucks on a rail to the kilns. Lime-burning stopped in 1875, but the kilns were still open in my younger days. Eventually they were boarded up for health and safety reasons. My father, who would try his hand at anything that made a shilling or two, was working in the lime-kiln at one time, fell asleep and was overcome by fumes, and was only just discovered in time to be carried out and saved.

Turning left into Granary Lane, the only houses there in my young days were a block of about six cottages, a row of red-brick cottages, called Otterview Terrace and further up the lane, about six cottages known as Jersey Cottages, all situated on the River Otter side, and still there. The first of the six cottages mentioned was occupied by Mr and Mrs Trayhurn who ran a laundry from an annexe at the rear of the building. Other houses were soon built after the First World War and were subsidized by the local council to help people purchase their own homes. They were known as Council Houses, although never owned by the council. On the corner of Stoneborough Lane was the old gasworks, built in 1867. On the opposite side stand two semi-detached houses, one of which, still called Whitemoor, I bought from J.W. Palmer who built it, for £447. I mention this because then, in the 1930s, we looked out over the two old gasometers, since demolished, but now there is a lovely view over the top of the Council Houses to the estuary and beach as far as the Otter Head, one of the loveliest parts of the bay. I called the house Whitemoor because that was the name of the small farm where my wife was born, in Iddesleigh, near Winkleigh, mid-Devon.

Passing along toward the seafront, on the right was a little house, now the site of Mimosa Court, occupied by the manager of the gasworks. It was called Fluvia. I think the manager had a sense of humour, as the smell from the near-by gasworks was at times overpowering. Just beyond, on the left, were three cottages in a lane leading to other houses, and a yard used as a coal depot. The coal depot still stands but the cottages have all been demolished. They were often flooded in the winter months, and were in a very unhealthy position, although the occupants perhaps would not have agreed with that. The River Otter used to have much more water before a lot of it was diverted for Taunton. Coal used to be landed at this end of the beach until 1885, when it was considered more convenient to bring it in from Exmouth, which had a newly built railway. Also grain used to be landed near the Otter mouth and stored in a granary in this area – from which came the name of Granary Lane.

Proceeding back towards the lime-kilns we pass the entrance to the cricket field and pavilion. Next to the cricket field, on higher ground, is now the car park. It was a small affair, compared to what it is now, and made by tipping refuse on to the marshland. The car park is bounded at the east side by the public footpath that leads to a delightful walk along the river bank to Otterton, and then on to Newton Poppleford, and indeed further still. The stream that runs parallel with the path and then underneath the road and beach is the brook that comes from Kersbrook and wanders along the Little Marshes on the west side of the estuary to the sea.

But back to the seafront and along the cliffs towards the town. These cliffs are of a soft sandstone, and one can spot a number of plants in their natural surroundings; thrift or cliff daisies, as they are known locally, and spectacular masses of mesembryanthemums or Livingstone daisies, in places reaching the height of the cliff! In a recent television programme entitled 'The Cliffs of Britain', the camera focused on a ridge of pebbles which I instantly recognized, and then on to the cliff face, and before the commentator mentioned Budleigh Salterton, I knew at once this particular section of cliffs. When I was recently at a garden centre a long way from Budleigh Salterton, I saw some pebbles which an artist had tastefully painted with flowers and animals etc. I knew they came from my home town, but to make sure I made enquiries, and my word, wasn't I thrilled when I was told they had been found in Budleigh Salterton! Even in my time painted pebbles like these were sold in Budleigh Salterton, often at bazaars, as paperweights. I was also told then, although I had heard it before, there is only one other place in the world where similar stones are to be found, and that is on a beach in Brittany.

Originally there was no path under these cliffs,

Lower end of Granary Lane with the old gas works and cottages, often flooded in winter

The marshes and brook from Kersbrook

The Esplanade ended halfway along Marine Parade

The path at the foot of the cliff, made by throwing soil down from the cliff when the road was excavated

The boathouse and the newly constructed road

the esplanade ended halfway along Marine Parade. The first section of the path came about in 1885 when the Coastguard Cottages were built, and the present road, Coastguard Hill, made. The soil that was excavated was thrown over the cliff and then turned into a rough path. Before that, the pebbles used to come right up to the cliffs, like they do at the 'West End'. But in my young days the path had been extended all along under the cliffs, and there were two shelters and a boat-house. Here was kept the longboat which was manned by eight coastguards, four rowing each side when they went out to assist vessels in distress, or to intercept smugglers. The old boat-house is now a café, and where on the beach there used to be nothing,

Bathing Station and bathing 'machines'

there are now rows of beach huts; not very pretty to the eye. The beach huts never used to obstruct the pedestrian's view, the bathing machines and any huts being situated nearer the town and on the pebbles closer to the water's edge.

The Bathing Station on the Marine Parade was started by a man called Daniel Middleton in the 1880s. He started with three bathing machines, which later on were run by a Scot called Archie Forbes. He increased their number to seven by the early 1900s. Very grand affairs they were, hexagon-shaped, on four massive wheels, the two wheels nearest the sea much larger than the other two, to allow for the slope of the beach.

Anyone who has not seen this type of bathing machine cannot realise what a marvellous sight they were with their panelled sides painted blue and white. As the tide fell they were lowered to the water's edge, ladies inside, so that they could step into the sea without being seen. It was considered improper, almost immoral, to be seen not fully dressed – even though the costumes of that time covered far more of the person than does the normal dress worn by the ladies of the present generation. Later, the bathing-machines, with ladies inside, would be pulled up again – with the help of a capstan – being made of oak the bathing machines were very heavy.

The Gooding's capstan on the Esplande

The bathing costumes had full length sleeves, with a cape like a sailor's collar worn over them, and extended from the shoulders down to the ankles. Stockings and rope-soled bathing shoes protected the feet from the pebbles. There was a length of rope attached to each machine, and the ladies would wade out to about waist deep and bob up and down in the water until they were fully wet. Few ladies could swim in those days, and no wonder! It would have been practically impossible in those costumes. They were made in a heavy serge material, usually navy blue, with white braid trimmings to hide the shape of the body.

At the West End of the beach, under the cliffs, a different kind of bathing was going on; nude bathing, but for a reason the present generation cannot imagine. Working-class people of those days simply could not afford to buy bathing costumes for themselves or their children. So men and boys went swimming the way they were made. The story goes that a lady in The Parade complained that she could see nude men from her window; in response to this the bathers were banished further west. After this, she still complained that she could see them – through her binoculars! There was a notice on the board at the bottom of the Steamer Steps forbidding nude bathing east of that point. It was there until 1917 when the board was swept away in a storm.

During my early years the bathing machines came into my father's possession. It happened like this; Archie Forbes, for some reason, left the town rather hurriedly, owing Dr Semple, in whose cottage he lived in Ryll Lane, £80. I remember my father receiving a message to call on Dr Semple that evening, and no one could think of a reason for the summons. However, when he arrived Dr Semple offered my father the bathing machines, for the sum of £80, to recover his debt, although in those days they would have fetched a much higher price. My father pointed out that he had not got anything near that sum of money. He was told it was not expected that he would be able to pay at once, and on that condition he accepted the offer. From these beginnings the Bathing Station, as it became known, developed.

Tents at the Bathing Station. Notice the ladies on the path with the maid pulling the bath-chair

In its heyday there were, besides the original seven machines, about fifty changing tents at the Bathing Station. The tents were made of unbleached twill, sewn by members of the Gooding family themselves, and had wooden floors which were scrubbed daily with disinfectant. If people had not brought their bathing costumes and towels they could hire them. There were also two refreshment huts, or 'tea huts', as we called them, and over 200 deck chairs, some with a canopy attached. The charge for a deck chair was 2d. for three hours, or 3d. if it had a canopy. The chairs were taken to any part of the beach the customer fancied, and they often had to be fetched back from the river mouth area. The charge for a cup of tea was 2d.; a pot of tea on a tray with a sugar basin, milk jug and cup and saucer, in fluted bone china, with bread and butter and two cakes, was 11d. Trays and crockery were often left on the beach after use, sometimes below the high-water mark. Surprisingly, losses and breakages were very rare, and, if reported, were never charged for.

With my two older brothers, I worked in this business for about twenty-five years and enjoyed every minute of it, although sometimes, if the weather was rough we were badly off financially. The business took a hard knock for two or three years after the First World War when two young ex-servicemen started a rival concern; The West End Bathing Station, near the Rolle Hotel and the Steamer Steps. It was nearer the town, and peoples' sympathy in those times was for the ex-servicemen. My father and I, just a young lad then, did our best. Eventually my two brothers came to our rescue and we ran the business under the name of Gooding Bros. The tents were gradually replaced by wooden huts which my brother Bill constructed himself. He also built a raft for the bathers, a very solid affair which, on occasion, proved troublesome because certain young men from the big houses used to play a prank on us by overturning it. One evening, when everybody had gone, we painted tar underneath the raft and that put an end to the pranks.

I remained with my brothers until the outbreak

West End Bathing Station which started just after the First World War

Gooding Brothers Bathing Station

The bathing raft built by Bill Gooding

of the Second World War when the huts were cleared off the beach and stored for the duration. But the old bathing machines, which had not been moved for years, were smashed and removed by the army. Pleas were made to the officer commanding the operation that the machines might perhaps, be preserved. But no, they had to be removed at once. And so a landmark that had been a feature of the beach since Queen Victoria's reign was lost for ever. When the beach was returned to the public, my eldest son ran the business with one of my brothers until the beach was taken over by the council.

On the land side, overlooking the Bathing Station, there was an imposing house, Eastcliff, standing a little above the level of the road. The gabled upper storey was removed in later years, which transformed the appearance of the house completely. The next four houses and the Southlands Hotel, or rather the eastern end of the hotel, is all that remains of this part of Marine Parade as it was, until the modern trend for pulling down the old buildings and removing the old features started, not always with pleasing results. The old part of the hotel is easily recognized, being quite different in appearance. It was known as Eastbourne Villa and was run as a boarding-house by Mr Webber and his two sons; the old man looked like a character from a Charles Dickens novel. The Southlands Hotel became important because of its position near the beach, and in the 1920s it counted among its guests quite a number of titled persons who, instead of going to bathe in the sea, had sea water carried in buckets into the hotel and poured into the bath. This was a welcome opportunity to earn additional money, for you were paid 1d. a bucket, which was not bad. The guests would come in their own carriages, with horses and grooms, and the ladies were attended by maids, and their children by nannies.

Next to Eastbourne there were two lovely villas with verandahs and pretty gardens in front. They have given way to 'progress', houses fronted by bleak concrete leading up to garage doors. Then comes a Victorian-looking house, which in my time was known as St Luke's. A gentleman called the Revd Wallace lived there

Marine Parade with the original Eastcliff House at the far end and St Lukes in the middle

Marybank with its elaborate verandah and iron railings

with two servants to look after him. After his death one of the maids showed me his false teeth, and that was the first time, to my recollection, I ever saw a set of teeth outside a human mouth. They were awesome-looking and very yellowed, and the palate was made of some brick-red substance, top and bottom being joined by a spring on either side. I mention this to emphasise how different things were in those days.

Again all the houses from St Luke's onwards are of 'modern' design until we get to South Parade, the first house there being built of brick

and therefore called Red House. It has been rendered since and is now called the Lighthouse. The Red House was occupied by Miss Burch who ran it as an apartment house. She could be seen dressed in the height of fashion, despite her age, and was always accompanied by her little black dog with its stump of a tail. I don't know what breed it was, but certainly it was no mongrel. Nothing so common place would have done for 'Lady-go-likely', as Miss Burch was often referred to, when not within hearing.

The next two houses, after the Red House, are old. Lochiel Lodge on the corner of the cul-de-sac, was a small apartment house run by Mr and Mrs Curry. This was I suppose, a superior establishment, in that Mr Curry was by trade a waiter, and usually served the meals himself. But also he was sometimes employed by Lord Clinton at Bicton House for special occasions, such as the visit of the Prince of Wales, later King Edward VIII, the Duke and Duchess of York, (now the Queen Mother), and Sir Winston Churchill. Mr Curry had been a waiter for Sir Oliver Morrison Bell, who resided at Harpford and was MP for the Honiton Division.

The old cul-de-sac on South Parade has changed completely. At the end was the old

South Parade with the Red House, Lochiel Lodge, the Octagon and the Gentlemen's Club

bathing machine yard, used for storing the machines during the winter months. Just above this was Ryll Cottage, since demolished, with a lovely sea view. The entrance was in Ryll Lane, a footpath joining South Parade and the junction of Fore Street Hill and East Terrace. When we were children we would often walk through the lane to look into the sitting-room window of the cottage, where a watch could be seen going under water, in a goldfish bowl. To us it was a wonderful sight.

On the left of the cul-de-sac was a pair of semi-detached apartment houses, Glenn Garth and Billbrook Cottage. At their rear was a dear little cottage, since demolished, which should have been left standing, as it was a lovely example of the buildings of the old town.

One of my duties when young was to do errands for my sisters, who were in service at several big houses in the town. After my oldest sister Alice had been in the same house in Station Road for some time, she decided to leave and started a small apartment house, or boarding residence as it was sometimes called, in this same cul-de-sac. On the advice of Mrs Curry she continued to wear 'uniform', which consisted of a print dress and apron for morning duties, and a black frock and more 'dressy' apron for afternoon wear.

One dark and stormy evening, when it was raining and blowing a gale, I was sent by my sister to W.W. Daniels to collect some afternoon aprons on approval. She had selected the ones she required, and I had to return the unwanted ones. She would call and pay for the ones she had kept when she was in the town. At the shop the aprons were put into a dress box with a lid and a strap that went over the shoulder, a type of container used in most cases by shopkeepers' errand boys. Mr Daniels reminded me to be careful as it was such a bad night, and all went well on the first part of the journey. The selection was made, and the remainder repacked carefully between layers of tissue paper. On the return journey to Daniels, disaster struck. About halfway across the bridge I tripped and fell headlong, the box opened and the contents scattered all over the road. Imagine if you can the state of the roads, which were not tarmaced in those days, but covered in loose gravel. All traffic was horse-drawn and the road-sweepers had finished work some time

before. I was horrorstruck, and, on impulse, tossed the aprons back into the box and returned to Daniels. I handed the box to Mr Daniels and said 'Alice will call and pay later' and was out of the door before you could say 'W.W. Daniels'. I slept rather fitfully that night and feared the anger of my father when the truth would come out, as it must do before long. I got away to school next morning without anything being said, and although I hoped for the best, I knew in my heart I should have to answer for it soon. When I arrived home from school my father called me to him and said, 'Mr Daniels wants to see you. Have you any idea what he wants?' My heart pounding, I said, 'No, I didn't'. He said, 'You had better go and see him'. This I did, making the journey last

South Parade in 1914, showing the brook and the bridges that crossed it

as long as I could. On going into the shop, Mr Daniels took me into a back room and told me I had done wrong not to tell him what had happened, and that as I went through life, I should always own up and tell the truth, even if, as in this case, it was a pure accident – something I have tried my best to do and keep my promise to him. My father never mentioned the incident again, although my conscience did for sometime. Neither did I get the punishment I expected, which I like to think was due to a request from Mr Daniels, who might have thought that he had dealt with me sufficiently. Forty years or more later, I was at a meeting of the Freemasons' Lodge at Budleigh Salterton, when Mr Daniels was present. He caught my eye and seemed to say, 'I see you have taken my advice, or you would not be sitting where you are today'.

But back to our walk. The remainder of South Parade to where it joins The Square is just the same as it used to be; there is The Octagon, famous as the house where in 1870 Sir J.G. Millais painted the picture of the boyhood of Sir Walter Raleigh. Then comes Fairlynch, which is now the local museum. It was built, so the story went, by a retired sea captain who put in the turret as a look-out to remind him of his days at sea, but I am told that this isn't true. On the opposite side is the Gentlemen's Club, whose car park was a patch of pebbles and grass – a play patch for children, gone forever, I fear. The wall flanking this car park was known as the Quay Wall, and countless numbers of children must have walked on it and sat on the 'mushroom' at the end. I wasn't a gentleman and knew little of what went on inside the club, but I understand that there was a well-furnished billiard room, a card and reading room and a bar.

On entering The Square the road now veers left into Fore Street. But this was not so in my youth. Then the road ran along close to The Glen and ended at a T-junction, with the right turn up Fore Street Hill and the left turn across the brook over a narrow bridge, where it turned right into Fore Street. The brook went under the bridge and continued through the middle of what is now

The old road ran close to The Glen and Round Corner, and then veered left over the bridge into Fore Street

The Square, leaving a large area in front of the houses on the seaward side. This area, being traffic free, was used for various purposes; whether public meals on occasions such as coronations, or for the setting up of stalls for the sale of goods on charity days, such as Alexandra Rose Day. Traffic was mainly horse-drawn, so tables and stalls would be set up in any wider part of the street, for instance in Fore Street opposite Perriams the grocers. The brook is now covered from The Square to the Gentlemen's Club, which has made the road wider, but that is all that can be said for it! Before the traffic was diverted at the top of High Street into Station Road, to join the East Budleigh Road at Stoneborough, all buses and other traffic came through the town along Marine Parade and Coastguard Hill, which at times caused considerable congestion. For a time, buses from Sidmouth were allowed through the town but that, too, was discontinued.

We will now continue our walk up Fore Street Hill. At the bottom on the left used to be two shops. The first one, where Corner Cottage is

now, was a little shop owned by Maria Farrant, who sold a mixture of goods from sweets to Honiton lace. Next door was a general store-cum-off-licence, with china and glass as an added attraction, run by Mrs Tom Hitt. She lived with her family in a farmhouse in Chapel Street, next to the Salterton Arms. Next came a double-fronted house with workshops in the rear yard, where local carpenter and joiner, Mr Cowd, used to make amongst other things, coffins to order.

You are now in Poplar Row. The whole road has been rebuilt, and although it is still a quiet retreat, it has lost the 'olde-worlde' appearance it used to have. Continuing up Fore Street Hill we come to the junction of East Terrace and Ryll Lane, and here the walls on either side are built of rock taken from the shore east of the River Otter. In Ryll Lane on our right, is Pear Tree Cottage. Workmen, while looking for a new path for a soakaway, unearthed a hole some 8 feet square by 6 feet deep. Various suggestions were made as to its original purpose, including a smugglers' hole for a brandy cache. The hole was

Turning into Fore Street Hill. Notice Mount Pleasant Cottage on the left, now gone

not filled in permanently, but filled with stones, and a slab placed over it, so that it could be reopened in the future.

Back in Fore Street Hill, the cottages and houses on our right are among the oldest in the town, built around 1700. Most of them have undergone numerous transformations in the course of time, and only Hillcroft on the bend is still thatched. Little Hill was, in the second half of the eighteenth century, the seaside residence of General Graves Simcoe, governor of Upper Canada, and the house thereafter was called Simcoe House. During my time, there was a surgery in this house, and Fore Street Hill was known to everybody until the 1960s as Surgery Hill. The yard with the garages, through which Little Hill is approached, used to be the stabling and coach-house for Lion House next door, a very stately Regency house, so named because of the lions mounted on pillars at the entrance to the drive. When we were children we were told that when the lions heard the clock of the Temple (the original name of the Methodist church) strike the midnight hour they would jump down from the pillars and go down the hill to the brook for a drink. This used to terrify us as we were told that

it was true. What we did not understand was that it all depended on the word 'heard'. Opposite Little Hill, on a triangular plot perched above the road, a few feet behind a rock wall, stands a large house called Grey Garth. A few years after it was built disaster struck. After a very wet spell the retaining wall collapsed, leaving the house in danger. Immediate repairs were started, and in a few weeks it was considered safe again. On the west side of Grey Garth, about halfway up the slope behind No 1 East Terrace, there used to be a cottage called Mount Pleasant. It was demolished, but its foundations and part of the walls can still be seen, surrounding a little garden.

Opposite Lion House a lane runs up the hill around the grounds of Elvestone. It leads to the old cricket field and continues as a pathway to Upper Chapel Street. On this path is the entrance to Umbrella Cottage, a very old house formerly known as The Cottage, worth noting because of the umbrella-shaped roof of the porch. When the excavations at Pear Tree Cottage were reported in the *Exmouth Journal*, reference was made to a tunnel between Fairlynch and this cottage. Past Lion House is Madeira Walk, from which a lovely view over the bay can be seen. It was just a rough

The Cottage, now known as Umbrella Cottage

lane in my time, locally known as Poppy Ground or by some people, Lovers' Walk.

Now to return to the Square. Around 1920 The Glen and Round Corner, which was then a small dairy, were offered, together with Fairlynch, for sale by auction. My father, who had been keen to own a freehold house, asked the manager of Lloyds Bank, Mr Penny, what chance there would be to borrow the amount he needed. He was told to go ahead. As he did not have enough for a deposit, it was a big venture both for my father and the bank. He went to the auction, and The Glen was knocked down to him for his bid of £500 – a small price even in those days for a house with three reception rooms and five bedrooms. And it's position couldn't have been better. Round Corner was sold for the same price, and Fairlynch for £900.

On the other side of The Square, the building in the corner, now a private house, was the Conservative and Unionist Club. Next door was the police station, now known as The Old Clink. There was little freehold property in the town. The Rolle Estate owned most of the property in Budleigh Salterton, and the only freehold in the town area were the houses from the police station to the Gentlemen's Club and from The Octagon to Round Corner, with Fairlynch in between.

Fore Street, as far as the Rolle, has undergone a lot of change. On the seaward side it was almost an uninterrupted row of shops, many rented rather than owned by the people who ran them. The shops were open from 8 a.m. to 7 p.m., Saturday 9 p.m., and early closing was on Thursday at 5 p.m. People used to work between 60 and 70 hours or more a week. Around 1914 a great many leases ran out and reverted to the Rolle Estate. Many of the leading businesses had moved to High Street, where there was still quite a lot of residential accommodation. After the leases ran out, many of the old buildings were pulled down and replaced, rather piecemeal, by the present ones, not always with a pleasing effect. There was a scheme devised by 'Alfie' Carter of Exmouth to replace all the buildings in the area with chalet bungalows both for residents and holiday-makers and an arcade where people could do their shopping, in the dry. It didn't come about; Alfie never returned from the battlefields in France.

Back in The Square, the tall red-brick building with intricate terracotta floral designs and faces,

Looking up Fore Street when it was Budleigh's main shopping Street. The first building on the left became the Police Station, and the building next door was replaced by the tall red brick house, 'Walter's Folly'

next door to The Old Clink, was, in my young days a butcher's shop, and although I do not remember it, they used to drive the animals for slaughter through the shop to the slaughterhouse at the end of the yard. Each butcher used to have his own slaughterhouse, and the boss or his senior employee used to do their own slaughtering. They also bought and sold animals. For that purpose they either owned or rented fields to run their cattle, and such fields were known by the name of the butcher who owned or rented them. I mentioned Webber's Field in Coastguard Road; it was owned by butcher Webber. The red-brick building was originally built for Mr Walters, and because he built it so tall it was always known to locals as Walter's Folly.

The shop next door although much altered, is one of the very few surviving really old buildings on this side of Fore Street. It used to be a grocer's shop, and it was here that I bought my first packet, or rather bag, of potato crisps, for 1d. They were made by a firm called Carters, who were in business long before Smith's Crisps went on sale. Next to that was a draper's shop which bore on the fascia the inscription 'P. Henry Gush', and was, in spite of its position at the end of the shopping area, the leading business of its kind in the town, and its annual sale was one of the major events.

A little further along was an old established ironmonger's called T. Beer. Modern shopping habits caused the closure of this shop, and that of three or four similar shops in the town. There is a story that one day Mr Sedgemore ('Curly'), went into Beer's with his wife to buy some corrugated iron sheets to roof a shed he had built. The manager, Bertie Stamp, asked them in the usual way 'Can I help you?' Before Curly could say anything, Jemima said, 'Us wants two or three sheets of 'crinkly tin''. Seeing the puzzled look on his face, Curly said, 'Donee tek no notice of 'ur, Mr Stamp. What us wants is some of thikee there consecrated iron'.

As there was no telephone at the Bathing Station my brother Fred used to give Mr Stamp's telephone number to people, especially those from Exeter, who would ring on a Wednesday afternoon (early closing in Exeter) to inquire what the weather was like before coming to Budleigh Salterton.

Next door, Mr Challis, known to all as 'Jacker' Challis, ran, in my early days, a greengrocer's shop. He was also a poulterer. Jacker Challis was another of the colourful town characters, famed for his tenor voice, but also for not paying his poultry suppliers very promptly! One day, the story goes, he got himself locked up in a chicken run by a farmer's wife, who would not let him out until he had paid for her last supply. He owned a very tired-looking horse and carriage, which he used for general passenger trade, meeting trains, especially on Friday evenings, and a small flat wagon for the carriage of luggage and other goods. But he did not seem to be very proficient at it! The horse, like its owner, was fast coming to the end of its useful life, and both moved very slowly. On one occasion Jacker was going on a local trip, and my brother Fred, who was always noted for his wit, was going the same way. He was offered a lift but said, 'No thank you Mr Challis, I'm in a hurry'. You will note that he called him Mr Challis, not Jacker, no doubt as a result of his early training in giving adults proper respect. Jacker stabled his horse and some donkeys and also kept his vehicles in a cul-de-sac off Chapel Street, within a few yards of a fish-and-chip shop owned by 'Buckett' Sedgemore.

Next came a lodging-house, with a bay window, run by Miss Williams, nicknamed 'Tripp'. Then, on the corner of Parks Lane, Miss Cowd, known to all as 'Zilla', ran a milliner's shop; it was not a very profitable establishment, so she went in for sports articles and bric-a-brac as well. She used to attend all the house sales in the district and would always, whatever the article, whether it be a saucepan or a piano, start the bidding with a shilling. On the other corner was a jeweller's shop owned by a man called Boyce. It later became a branch of the newly formed Co-op. Next came a private house, Osmunda, so called I think for the lovely display of *Osmunda regalis* fern which adorned the front. This also was a boarding-house and was run by Mrs Mann, the wife of a very respected town councillor, an office which merited much more respect than it would in these times. The single-fronted house next door was another grocer's shop, run by a man known to everybody as Sid Cowd; whose sons carried on the business in the last shop in the High Street after their first shop had been pulled down. Next door, where The Pebbles is now, was an old house which, like the present one, lay back a little

The shop where Jim Gooding bought his first packet of potato crisps. It is now altered beyond recognition

The shops in Fore Street as they were in the 1920's–30's. P. Henry Gush, T. Beer, and after a private house, Zilla Cowd's bric-a-brac shop followed on the other side of Park Lane, by the Co-op

from the road. It was known as the Coffee Tavern, but later turned into Marine Hotel, with lovely gardens front and back. The Revd Boucher, who was instrumental in building the Cottage Hospital, was generous in many other ways. He would give vouchers for food to children he thought were in need of an extra meal, and these vouchers could be exchanged for food at the Coffee Tavern. In the early days of the First World War, I can remember a large hoarding erected in the front garden with a picture of Lord Kitchener pointing a finger at the passer-by. It bore the caption, 'Your King and Country Need You'. The finger pointed straight at you and followed you around, until out of sight.

The next building, jutting out a little on to the pavement, was a chemist's shop owned by a very old man called Sanders, who was always known as 'Ching Chang' Sanders. Why, I can't imagine. As far as I remember, he bore no resemblance to a Chinaman. He also was a dentist, and in spite of the notice which said 'Teeth extracted with greater facility and less pain than is usually anticipated', many gruesome tales were told of patients being dragged around the shop by the pincers. There was no surgery, and extractions were performed in the shop.

There was a passage between this shop and 19 Fore Street. At the end of the passage, on the left, was the side entrance to the chemist's shop, and the garden entrance to a charming 'olde worlde' cottage where some people called Spillers ran a laundry, and during the summer months, they used to dry the white linen on the beach in the bright sunlight. No 19 was our home for a few years and deserves a special mention. It used to be a double fronted shop, occupied by a shoemaker-repairer, and the wide passageway led through to the back area which was shared with the owners of the next two shops. This passage was open at the yard end, which in turn led to sheds and stabling and the owner, at that time, used to keep a donkey there. There were

Fore Street with the Coffee Tavern sign, later it became Marine Hotel (above left)

'Ching Chang' Saunders' Pharmacy in Fore Street

two toilets shared between the three premises situated right at the end of the outbuildings. There was no water supply but there was a pump in the yard at the back of the third shop, and all water had to be pumped by hand and carried to the house. The second shop was occupied by a tailor, Mr Linscott, a white-bearded old man whose workshop was at the back of the yard, and there was a covered way between his back door and the workshop. The third shop was very small with a window that could have been used to illustrate a novel of Charles Dickens. Here, two old ladies sold sweets and a variety of cheap toys, mostly of German origin. If they were examined closely, the markings of the old tin cans they were made of could be seen on the inside. The ladies were Miss Duneford and Mrs Crabtree who was never seen outside the shop. To us children Miss Duneford was always referred to as 'Miss Toyshop'.

The very first building on the left (only partly visible) was the Gooding Fish & Vegetable shop; next came Mr Lindscott's shop, followed by Miss Duneford's 'Toy shop', Lloyds' Bank, Perriams and Pidsley the Baker (later Parker's)

Perriam's; the high-class grocer and provision merchant, which has now also gone

The three properties were replaced by the modern building now owned by Prior's. Lloyds' Bank, still there, came next, and then Perriam's, a very old-established family concern. Like other high-class grocers, this shop had a 'Rapid Wire Cash Carrier' system, pear-shaped or pepper-pot like containers on overhead wires which ran from various points at the counter to the cash desks. It saved the assistant the walk to the desk with the customer's money, where he might have to wait for the change, and he could serve the next customer while the cashier dealt with the money. Perriam's used to make their own blocks of ice, mineral water and ginger beer etc., but like many other high-class grocers and provision merchants, the shop has changed to a serve-yourself mini-supermarket, a change the older generation have never liked or got used to. My own impression is of being watched and suspected from the time you enter until you have passed through the check-out.

The last shop on this side of the road was Parker's, the bakers'-cum restauranteur, complete with bakehouse at the rear. All the bread etc. was baked on the premises, as was the case with the other principal bakers in the town. In fact they did not only bake their own bread, but also the bread of Budleigh Salterton housewives, who made their dough and waited until a loud bell was sounded – it could be heard all over the town – a signal that the oven was ready. They then came along to have their bread baked. Parker's was a very successful establishment and renowned for, among other things, their Russian Square, (a kind of Battenburg). One day old Mrs Pidsley was heard to shout, 'Tommy, you'll have to cut this Russian Square smaller. We're selling too many!' Mr Parker, who took over the business when his wife's parents, Mr and Mrs Pidsley, retired, also had other interests, including a small poultry farm in Upper Stoneborough Lane. He also attended to the many chocolate machines on the seafront and at other vantage points in the town. They were operated by placing one penny in the slot and on pulling out the drawer the machine would release a bar of chocolate, usually Nestlés, which was, in those days, good value. I am sorry to admit that the young people soon found a trick for 'milking' the machines, which, until a way was found to stop it caused poor Mr Parker a lot of worry. Parker's restaurant was famous locally for a very special ice cream which was expensive even in those days.

The next building was the Rolle Hotel, one of the most prominent buildings of the town, and centre for many public events, whether gatherings to listen to speeches on Empire Day, coronations, elections, or open-air services of various descriptions. The hotel was a first-class family and residential establishment, with large entrance hall, lounge, coffee, smoking and billiard rooms. The lawn facing the sea was large enough for either two tennis courts, or a bowling green and croquet lawn. The hotel had its own ostlery and mews across the road, providing transport with landaus and wagonettes etc. for their guests. As special privileges, guests were offered trout-fishing tickets for the River Otter, and favoured terms for the golf links. The house was

Rolle Hotel before the First World War

Sea front aspect of the Rolle Hotel with extensive lawns

51

altered and enlarged several times during the hotel boom between the wars, I am afraid not always with pleasing results. With the loss of this hotel Budleigh Saltertion lost one of its finest assets, and the town has never been the same since.

We will now cross the street. The first shop on the corner of Chapel Street was a dairy, and, like all dairies of the time, sold only milk, cream, butter and eggs. It was owned by Mr and Mrs Barns. Inside, in a prominent place, there was a picture showing a mooing cow. Mrs Barns used to sit in the shop in a big black taffeta dress with a bottle of gin under her skirt. Mr Barns was responsible for the delivery of milk, which was measured from a large can, or in the case of delivery by horse milk-float, from an urn, which was in most cases an ornamental affair of well-polished steel and brass. Sad to relate, Mr Barns, together with Mr Larcombe, another dairyman, used to frequent the Feathers Hotel on completion of the morning round and was seldom in a fit state to attend to the afternoon delivery. Instead this was done by a couple of lads after school, but was only to a few selected customers and not so important. On his way home on such an occasion Mr Barns is reported to have kept saying to a companion, 'Isn't it a pity'. After a while curiosity caused his companion to inquire,

'What's a pity?'. The answer came in a mumble, 'Isn't it a pity that George Larcombe drinks'.

Next door to the dairy was another of the many apartment houses, followed by a tobacconist's and barber's, a combination of trades often found in those days. The barber's shop or saloon was in a room at the rear, a sort of conservatory, and it is still in existence today, but not as a gentlemens' hairdressers. It was built over the brook which runs at the rear and can be seen by walking along to the end of the block. Children used to be able to get a haircut for 1d., but I don't think that many children of today would be satisfied with the style. I was gone fourteen when I decided I would like something different, but barber Cowd, nicknamed 'Monty', said, 'I don't remember your father telling me you could do so', and proceeded to put the clippers over my head as usual. Needless to say, that was the last time he cut my hair. I used to go to Vickeray's after that and pay 2d.

Next door to the barber's was another dairy, but with a difference. Mr Smale was a dairy farmer who sold the milk from his own cows. He also sold other goods, all produced on his own farm. 'Blampy' Smale, as he was known, also had an interest in the Rolle Mews, which was behind his shop. In later years, after Mr Sanders the chemist had retired, the town was left without a dentist, so Mr Smale let his front room as a

Next to Barns Dairy was an apartment house, followed by Cowd's Barber and Tobacconist, and at the end of the block the Rolle Dairy

Ash Villa, built by James Lackington in 1812. It was demolished in 1955

surgery to Mr Harrison, who had a practice in Exmouth and used to attend on a half day a week – a bit unfortunate if one had toothache on any other day. It was several years before there was a resident dentist in the town.

Next to the Rolle Mews was the garden belonging to Dr Semple of Abele Tree House, which is still there. However, its garden was taken away together with the Rolle Mews, to make the present car park. Abele Tree House was approached by a drive over the brook, which also was the entry to Ash Villa. Ash Villa and the Wesleyan Chapel, The Temple, were built by James Lackington in the first decade of the nineteenth century and Mr Lackington spent the last years of his life in this magnificent house. In my time Ash Villa was occupied by Mr and Mrs Ernie Sargent, and was run by Mrs Sargent as an apartment house. Ernie was a quaint little man, truly an old character of the times and deserves a special mention here. He was a painter and decorator by trade, but he had a passion for all

kinds of animals and birds. His back yard was a veritable menagerie, and among his many pets was a monkey called Jinnie. It was known to everybody in the town, and people living nearby had cause to remember it as it escaped on several occasions. Ernie would be hurriedly called from his work to try and capture Jinnie – no easy task – and often much mischief had been caused, such as pushing a bath sponge into a rainwater pipe, which was not discovered until the next downpour. Another of Ernie's pets was a billy goat which had been taken to a local butcher to be slaughtered. The butcher, being softhearted in spite of his profession, contacted Ernie, who adopted the goat and gave it the name of Joey. They could often be seen when Ernie took Joey to some quiet spot for grazing, a much easier task then as the roads were far less dangerous. Ash Villa became the Temple Methodist Manse after Ernie left, but this beautiful house, too, fell victim to 'progress' and was pulled down in 1955 to make way for the present car park.

The lawn on the other side of the entrance to the Methodist Church is the former site of a house with a shop. When I first knew it, it was an ironmongers' which later moved to more spacious premises in the High Street. The house, then occupied by Mr and Mrs Whalley, is remembered for a disaster. During a gale the end and part of the frontage collapsed and an old lady called Mrs Baker, who was a lodger, was catapulted out into the front garden, still in bed, and was only saved from going into the brook by a thick hedge that bordered it. Accommodation was hurriedly obtained for Mr and Mrs Whalley and their family, and Mrs Baker was taken in by her daughter.

Next to this house was a bridge over the brook which led to Pebble Lane and, in turn, to Poplar Row and East Terrace. On the other side of the bridge was a house with a shop, fronted by a wide verandah, then known as The Library. It sold all manner of goods, from books, artists' and photographic materials, picture-frames and stationery to toiletries. It was owned by Mr Dalglish, organist and choirmaster of St Peter's parish church. At the back of the premises was a small printing works operated by Mr C Horrell. Next to The Library came two shops with an open passage between them which was then the entrance to the Y.W.C.A., later moved to the High Street. The caretaker of the hostel was Mr Frank Sanders, who was also a painter and decorator, a trade in great demand in those days before DIY became so popular. Then followed a cottage, since rebuilt, and then another shop with a verandah, very similar to The Library, run by a dairy farmer called Arbury, nicknamed 'Lardy'. He had two daughters, and when told that they were now of marriageable age he replied, 'Don't you mention marriage to me. I have plenty of work for them to do'. The house next door and all the other premises were, as they are now, approached by bridges over the brook, which is still open in this section of Fore Street. The road then used to camber quite a bit and many a youngster including myself has fallen through the rails into the water.

We will now retrace our steps to Rolle Square, as it was known then. The High Street, although altered in character, has not undergone the same drastic changes as Fore Street, which is now mainly residential. We can begin with the two shops next to Rolle Road. There were originally three, a tobacconist, a baker, and a general haberdashery. The tobacconist was Mrs Mustow, a woman of gigantic proportions, who, on descending the three steps into the shop, was so breathless that she could hardly speak. Later this shop was shared by the Co-op, who used it as their first grocery shop until they moved to Fore Street, and still later back to High Street, where they are now. The baker's shop was owned by Mr Underhill, nicknamed 'Geordie', who was also a part-time fisherman. The haberdashery was run by an old couple called Marshall and their son, who inherited the business but who left the town to run a pub in another part of Devon when the building was demolished. On this site butcher Webber had his shop later on. Next door was Daniels' which looks exactly the same now as it did then, still selling a mixture of various articles, clothing, underwear, footwear and harberdashery. But no member of the Daniels family lives or works there now.

Next door to Daniels' was a shoe shop owned by Creedys', a very old established firm who still have premises at the top end of this block, by Cliff Road. The King William Hotel next to it was known to all as the 'King Billie' and appears to have altered little externally. Inside, I could not say. As far as I can remember, I only ever went into the off-licence, or 'jug and bottle' as it was referred to then. But I do remember that on top of the partition between the 'jug and bottle' and the public bar was a large stuffed thresher shark which had been caught locally.

The next part of the High Street has altered a lot. In my time Connett's outfitters was next door to the King Billie, followed by a shop front with arches, which was a corn-chandlery, forage merchants' and seedsman with the name of Raymont. There was considerable trading in this business, as most houses of any size, and of course the local shopkeepers, owned horses or ponies which had to be stabled and fed. The premises went back to Queen Street at the rear as did most of the shops in High Street. One only has to think that there was no motors in my early days, that all deliveries were by horse and cart or wagon, and the importance of establishments catering for their care and well-being is evident. Hooper's Stores, a name not very familiar now, came next, another family grocers' and off-licence. It was bought in 1939 by the Norman family, and carried on under the same name, while the son, W.K. Norman, started a wholesale service to hotels. When his father retired, the shop was sold and the wholesale business moved first to East Budleigh Road, once the premises of the town laundry, and then to the old railway yard. The next shop was a ladies outfitters by the name of Clatworthy. Later it became Hooker's fish shop. Then came Bickley the butcher, Creedy the outfitter, and then Beasleys', an

Glimpse of the house on the site of the present Methodist lawn between Ash Villa and the Library

View from Rolle Square of the shops on the left hand side of the High Street

Inside view of Hooper's Stores

Salterton Steam Laundry used to be in East Budleigh Road, now Norman's Furnishing Branch

artists' material shop owned by Tommy Ball, with the Y.M.C.A. above it. Finally there was Warren's Library, run by three sisters, one of whom would not hesitate to tell Dr Gavin, one of the towns family doctors, that some of the books he fancied were not suitable reading material for him!

From Warren's Library all the houses to the end of the block were rebuilt around 1912–13 and have changed little. Before this, next to Warren's, was a cottage and then came Blackburn's the photographers who also had a studio in Station Road at the beginning of Station Hill, long since gone. Blackburn's was an important establishment in those days, as there were very few cameras then, and those that were around were very large and heavy. Until the day of the Box Brownie, if you wanted 'your likeness taken', you had to go to Blackburn's.

Next to Blackburn's came No 18, which deserves a special mention, as our family went there to live when we left Poplar Row. My father had a shop front put in and a marble slab, and started a fish shop. When the block was demolished he took out the shop front and fittings, and moved them to 33 Fore Street, the house that used to be on the site of the present

The High Street before it was rebuilt in 1912–13. The Y.M.C.A., Beasley's and Warren's Library are on the left

Blackburn's the Photographers. Next to it is No 18, turned into a fishmongers by Eli Gooding. Mrs Gooding is in the doorway

Methodist Church lawn. There were two fishmongers in the town and about a dozen hawkers going from door to door with either a pony and trap, a handcart or just a basket on the arm; later on they had small motor vans. One day when my father was going around hawking herring (usually 6d. a dozen), the fish were rather larger than usual. He gave a customer only eleven for 6d., and when she queried this he said, 'There's not so many bigs 'uns to a dozen'. Next to No 18 were two pairs of cottages like those in Poplar Row, occupied by working-class families. One of the men was a workman for the council, and was known to all his acquaintances as 'Fixle Gold', pronounced 'Gould'. A house with a round corner brings us to the junction with Cliff Road.

Continuing along High Street, the next block starts with the Feathers Hotel, a commercial inn, which on the outside seems exactly as I remember it as a boy. It was run by Mr and Mrs Worth, but reached the peak of its fame when, after Mr Worth's death, Mrs Worth called in her three very attractive sisters to help run the establishment. One of them married J.W. Palmer, whose business is a little further up the High Street, and who was a frequent visitor to the inn. The Feathers Hotel had a 'Long Room' in Cliff Road, and anything important in the town used to take place at the Feathers. Next door was a newsagent called Thompson, shop front still the same as then, and the premises next door were the Imperial Dining-Rooms, a café run by Mrs Pleace, who also operated the telephone exchange. If a customer went into the shop and she happened to be at the switchboard, which was in the next room, they had to wait until she had finished 'pulling the call through'. You could hear her going through the lengthy business of 'Number please', and the whirring of the handle being turned. All telephones of that time were the same; handle on the side of the box-like instrument, mouthpiece protruding in front about six to eight inches, ear-piece hanging on a hook mounted to the wall, on the opposite side of the handle. To get a local call was fairly simple, but long-distance or trunk-calls could take as long as thirty minutes. Next to this café were two more cottages, demolished about 1910. This space is taken up by the Midland Bank and Marker's Café, formerly Marks' Café with bakery, and shop-cum-restaurant, which had a very elegant interior at

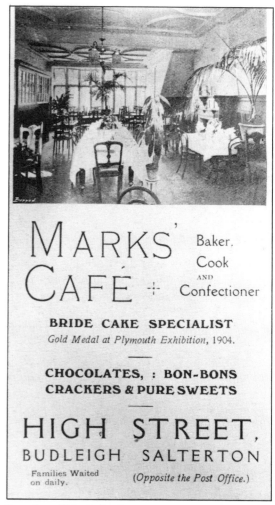

Interior of Marks' cafe

that time. It was run by Mr and Mrs Marks and their two daughters, and was so popular that there used to be a sign in the window that read, 'If you are in a hurry, do not come in'. Then came a china and glass shop, Newton Parsons, and next Palmer's, J.C. at that time, and later J.W. This firm played a very important part in the town. By the side of the shop was a long passage which was covered for about a quarter of its length and led to offices and a yard or garden. It was also the entrance to the rooms over the shop. This was quite unusual, as most shops were also entrances to the living quarters. A few had a side door leading to a passage which eventually led to the back rooms, or the staircase. At the end of

Palmer's passage one crossed a roadway which gave entrance from Victoria Place to several premises at the back of the High Street, including Marks' bakehouse. But its main purpose was to provide access to Palmer's yard. At the beginning of the working day numbers of workmen would be seen at the entrance to the passage in High Street waiting for the large bell to ring calling them to work, much the same as a factory hooter would do. This bell, known to all as Palmer's bell, could be heard at long distances and was generally accepted as correct time, as indeed it was. It was used as timekeeper for a lot of other workers of the firm, in whatever part of the town they were working. Between the First and Second World Wars Palmer's employed some two hundred people, mostly male, in the firm's various projects. You name it, Palmer's would do it for you, big or small, from furnishing a complete house to acting as funeral directors.

Next door was a ladies' and gents' hairdressers, which also sold cigarettes, tobacco and toiletries for ladies and gentlemen. Ladies' hairdressers were rare then and to my knowledge it was the only one in the town. Not so much money was spent on that sort of thing, and many years elapsed before home perms were available. The last shop on this side of the High Street was a butcher's, used later by the Cowd brothers as their new grocers' shop.

Next to this shop was a pair of dilapidated doors leading into a yard used as the firestation. The gardens of a pair of cottages took up the frontage to Victoria Place. The cottage next to the fire yard was lived in by Mr Cummings, who drove the fire engine. The story went, that when a fire was reported Mr Cummings would first go and inspect it to see how bad it was before calling out his men, all unpaid volunteers, and getting the fire engine out. He also owned a very old donkey, and grazed it in a field next to the vicarage. The field was used for fêtes then, but is now part of Meadow Road. Mr Cummings was a wheelwright and wagon builder, and his speciality was a box wheelbarrow for which he charged the sum of £1, ready-painted. Needless to say, practically every wheelbarrow for miles around bore his mark. The yard was shared between Mr Cummings and the council, who, besides using it to house the fire engine or engines of the time, also used it as a

Cottages at the top end of High Street. Notice the entrance to the Fire Yard opposite Moor Lane, now Station Road, and the Public Rooms in the background

The Salterton fire engine

Central Garage in the High Street

general depot. At this stage I must mention a very early model of fire engine. It was horse-drawn and operated by hand pump, three men on each side. It used to draw up water from any source available, and I can remember seeing it in action during a practice in Chapel Street by the brook which was then still an open stream. On this occasion it pumped water on to the roof of Prospect House in Upper West Terrace. But it was not long before a more modern version appeared on the scene.

The building on the opposite side of the street, on the corner of Station Road, is the National Westminster Bank, which opened in 1897. But I am told that it replaced a number of old cottage gardens fronting on to the road, and that the entire block was rebuilt before the turn of the century. Next to the bank was a chemists' called Shand's. One point I remember about the shop was its telephone number. Mr Shand must have applied for the telephone very early, as his number was Budleigh Salterton 1. Then came a shop owned by Mr Hutchings, a coach and charabanc builder who also sold bicycles. Mr Hutchings must have had great foresight, as he was one of the partners in a new venture, the

Central Garage, the other partner being Fred Sheppard. The garage was situated about half-way up the other side of High Street. Mr Sheppard also dabbled with wireless; on the occasion of the opening of Wembley Stadium in 1923, he installed a receiver on Hackley Field so that everyone could share in the marvel of hearing what was going on so far away. Next to Hutching's was the post office, which is very much the same outwardly, except that the door leading into the sorting office has been blocked up.

The premises between The Lawn and Rag Lane have had a complete face-lift of the frontages. Originally there were two pairs of imposing houses or villas there. But very early in my memory there was a shop, I think a haberdashery, on the corner of The Lawn. Behind the houses, at the end of Rag Lane, the scene has altered dramatically. Where the brook and a market garden once were, there is now no brook nor market garden, and the road continues over the closed-in brook to Chapel Street, affording rear entrances to the shops in the High Street. On the corner of Rag Lane, in the High Street, was Larcombe's Dairy, and next door to that, a private house once occupied by Mr and

Mr Sheppard's wireless receiver at Hackley Field, 1923

Mrs Pomeroy and now occupied by their daughter, Mrs Smith; it is the only private house left in High Street. It was followed by a fruiterer and greengrocers' above which, if I remember rightly, lived Mr Griffin, the headmaster of the school in Queen Street. In the next premises, Mr Harry Pratt ran his painting and decorating business; he used to specialize in wall-papering, quite an art in those days. In my boyhood, next door to Harry Pratt's was a small single-fronted cottage; after Mrs Mustow had given up her shop in Rolle Square, she transferred her business to here, but without putting in a shop front. She must have thought it a big improvement as there were no steps to negotiate. Next came a greengrocery-cum-dairy run by Mr and Mrs Pearce Gush, a dairy farmer whose cow shed and fields were around the Station Road area. Then came Keslake's bakers' shop, with bakehouse at the rear; and after that came a very small shop belonging to Mr Harry Hooker, who later, with his two sons, developed his business into a considerable wholesale and retail trade. Mr Hooker senior and Mr Tom Hooker, his son,

were both local councillors and magistrates. The honour of magistrate was conferred on each of them when they became chairman of the council, which they both were in turn, for several years. Following on we come to Pile's Greengrocery, a very old established shop. Mr Pile used to grow most of the produce himself in nearby fields. He had the nickname of 'Squirty' Pile because he was a very small man. Then came two red-brick houses which lay back from the frontage of the shops to give them a nice front garden. After that came a watch repairer and jeweller, George Coombes. The previous owner of the shop is reputed to have said when a customer called for a clock left for repair, 'Yes, it's ready, but it will take half-a-crown to make it go'. A reminder that he gave no credit! Then, Curtis the greengrocer's and florist's. George Curtis had a good reputation as a nurseryman and grew a large proportion of his flowers in hot-houses in Cliff Terrace. Then, two small cottages which have never been destroyed and add, in my opinion, to the attraction of the town.

There are only three more properties in High

Looking up High Street from Rolle Square. On the right, Staddon's Garage, which replaced George Bennet's Ironmongers shop, and Sid Keslake, the coal merchant's cottage have both since been demolished

Street to deal with. First, an ironmonger's owned by George Bennett, an old family of the town. After Mr Bennett's death the shop was turned into Staddon's Garage, another old family of the town. There was an entrance, next to this, to some cottages at the rear, fronting onto Brook Road, most of them demolished now. Next came the house of Mr Sid Keslake, a coal merchant who took the business over from his father, Ben Keslake. His cottage also was demolished only very recently. Sid owned one of the early commercial vehicles in the town, a Model T Ford which was used in many branches of transport, amongst others as the first town motor bus. Then he owned a taxi, a 'Sedan', followed by many more vehicles. The building on the corner of Chapel Street I can remember as Lloyds' Bank House. It was later turned into a grocer's shop, a branch of Wilson's Stores of Exmouth, and later still it became an antique shop.

While in this area we will proceed through Chapel Street, which has been altered beyond recognition, not, I fear, to its advantage. It used to be the 'Bond Street' of Budleigh Salterton. Just

Looking up Chapel Street

Looking down Chapel Street with Rolle Hotel in the distance

around the corner, at the rear of the bank premises, was a cottage built on the edge of the brook, which was still open at this time. I should think that at one time it had been a shop, as it had a large window. A very narrow passageway ran between this and the bank, which led to another pretty cottage with a small garden in front. It too was built on the edge of the brook. There was, and still is, a bridge, but the brook is now visible only near the back of the shops in Fore Street. Over the bridge on the left-hand side was a driveway leading to some stabling which housed the carriages and horses of one of the taxi services in the town, and to a block of houses, some private and some shops. One of the shops was a fruit and vegetable shop owned by Mary-Anne and Augie Webber. It had only one entrance from the pavement and would be known now as a 'lock-up' shop. In the area beside the shop the couple kept their small carts etc. and stabling for their donkey. It may seem strange to the present day reader, but then animals were allowed to be stabled quite near to living quarters and almost every working-class family used to have a few fowls in the garden or back yard. There was also an occasional pig and the consequent smell was always there. It was no wonder that the rat and mouse population was greater than the human population. Fleas were very numerous and continual warfare was waged on them, but not as successfully as now. The living conditions were against it and such conditions were accepted as normal.

But back to the street. Next to the driveway was a little general shop run by Mrs Jane Hill. There didn't seem to be much activity there, and how she and many more like her made a living is beyond my understanding. Then came two cottages to end the block, which had the appearance of being shops in earlier times. After these two cottages came Perriam's Place, which again has altered completely. On the left were the homes of several fishermen I have mentioned, among them Nelsie and Jim Rogers, who were looked after by their sister Bella. As their housekeeper, she tried hard to please them, which was no easy matter. The story goes that one morning at breakfast-time Bella was heard to shout up the stairs, 'Jim, breakfast be ready'. The reply came rather sleepily, 'Wot 'ave 'ee got'?

'Makell.'

'Be um boiled or fried?'
'Boiled.'
'Be um big or small?'
'Small.'
'Huh, I wouldn't give a cuss for a small makell boiled!'

A few days later a similar conversation was heard;

'Jim, breakfast be ready.'
'Wot 'ave 'ee got?'
'Makell.'
'Be um boiled or fried,'
'Fried.'
'Big or small?'
'Big.'
'Huh, I wouldn't give a cuss for a big makell fried!'

Poor Bella, she never did seem to get it just right. She was a hard-working woman; she used to cook the crabs her brothers caught, and went selling them, basket on arm, with the crabs wrapped in a cloth, and would rub them off with her apron as she went along. Three doors away at the end of the row of cottages lived the Pengilley family with two daughters, Edith and Ethel, and two sons Ernest and Stanley. Ernest was always known as 'Caker' and was very fond of whistling. Although not of fishing-stock, as a young lad he took to the beach and fishing, and his continual whistle used to get on Nelsie's nerves. On one occasion, after a prolonged performance, Nelsie said in an irritated voice, 'Why don 'ee shut up boy?'

Caker, hurt, said, 'I was only whistling a song, Nelsie'.

'Call that a song?', came the reply.

'Well, what would 'ee call a song?' asked Caker.

Came the reply, 'When I was young we used to sing songs like 'Annie Laurie' and 'Just like the Ivy that Clings to the Wall'. Nowadays all ee can 'ear is 'It ain't gonna rain no more, no more' and 'Horsey, cock your bloody tail up'.

To be fair to our generation, some lovely songs were written in our time, before the craze came for rag-time, beat and rock, and I suppose we now look upon the pop music of today with the same air of disdain.

Opposite these cottages was a rather larger one, and on either side smaller cottages running down towards the brook. The large cottage was lived in by Mr and Mrs Wesley Hitt, and their kitchen was large enough to hold concerts in aid

The old cottages in Bicton Terrace, known locally as Rogue's Roost

of the Mayor of Exeter's Farthing Breakfast Fund. The charge for admission was a halfpenny or a penny. The garden at the rear joined a meadow where cows used to graze and drink in the brook. There were several sheds in this garden and they were used to store blankets for the poor, which were lent out to them in the winter for 1d. or 2d. a week, and returned to be washed in the summer. The blankets were supplied by Mr Couch and his sisters, who were the landlords of Perriam's Place and lived in Chapel Street.

All those cottages have gone, and bungalows and some houses have been put up in their place. At the extreme end of the cul-de-sac was Sid Keslake's coal yard and stabling for his horses. On the corner of Perriam's Place and Chapel Street lived Frank Hill, a blacksmith, with shop and forge at the back of his cottage which fronted on to Chapel Street. There was always something interesting, to young and old alike, going on at the forge. Besides numerous horses and ponies to be

shod, all manner of ironwork would be made by him. A pastime for boys in the autumn was trundling a hoop made by the blacksmith, to whom they took it for repair when broken.

Further up Chapel Street was another cul-de-sac, with thatched cottages and a fisherman's store for nets and crab pots. The cottages, if suitably renovated, would now be considered a jewel in the town. But in those days few people thought of preservation. The store shed was in a corner of a yard which served for drying the family laundry from five houses. The name of this cul-de-sac was Bicton Terrace, but anybody local called it 'Rogue's Roost'. How it got its name I do not know, but seldom, if ever, was it called by its proper name. The cottages had linhays at the back which also served as wash-houses. The next house on the hill is a sort of lean-to against the last house on this side of Chapel Street, and you have to look carefully to notice at all that there is a separate entrance and house number to both places. The whole of it, beautifully and

65

symmetricaly built with unusual windows, is one of the prettiest surviving cottages of the town. The larger dwelling was the residence of Mr Couch, an eccentric old gentleman, and his two sisters.

Opposite the Couch residence was a garden belonging to a house in East Terrace. Further down the hill, approximately opposite 'Rogues Roost', was another group of cottages, rather attractive from the outside, with pretty windows and gardens in front. The first two had a shared entrance and were at right angles to each other. The third, facing the first one was lived in by Mr Archie Teed, town crier of Budleigh Salterton, and his wife. On special occasions Archie would go around the streets, with Walt Mears in a bearskin, much to the fright of the children. Another, rather larger house, double-fronted, made up the block. This was the farmhouse of Mr Tom Hitt, a dairyman who had cow sheds for about a dozen cows at the rear of the house. Milk, junket and cream were sold at the door. The sheds were rather ramshackle, and milking was done under conditions that would not be tolerated today. The cows were driven through the streets daily, as were two other herds owned by other farmers. In a short cul-de-sac beside the farmyard stood a small cottage, very noticeable by the fact that the walls were painted or rather tarred, black. And beyond this was another forge owned by Mr Jewell. On the other side of the cul-de-sac were more cow sheds belonging to Mr Challis. The stalls ran, in a long single row, down to the Rolle Mews, in fact they were part of it. They came later, on the removal of the cows to a farm in Knowle, into the possesion of the Salterton Arms, and were, much later, used as a store for beach huts etc. The Salterton Arms on the corner with its frontage in Chapel Street is adjoined by a small single-fronted cottage which was used by the landlord of the public house for his male employee. Following on we come to a double-fronted house which was, formerly, a shop or shops. After that came a small cottage, and then a shop which carried on several trades in turn. First it housed a shoe-repairer, then a general store run by 'Bucketts' Sedgemore and his wife. They also used what was then the wash-house, for frying fish and chips. The frying was done in the wash coppers, right next to some donkeys which Mr Challis stabled there, and the

Mr Tom Marker in the doorway of Cove Café

fish and chips – a halfpenny for the chips – were sold together with ice cream, from a handcart in Chapel Street. 'Bucketts' was an invalid who had to be pushed about in a bath-chair. After that Mrs Davie and her son then ran the shop as a greengrocers, until she moved to the newly-built shop in Fore Street which later became part of Prior's. Mr and Mrs Marker then opened the shop in Chapel Street as Cove Café, rather small for the twenty or so tables crammed in there. Orders for meals were often shouted to the kitchen door as there was so little room to move about. They later moved to Marks Café in High Street. Between this shop and the next one was an open-fronted driveway. The side doors of both shops and the entrance to the fish frying department were in this driveway. A covered yard led to the Rolle Mews and Challis's cow

1–5 East Terrace, red brick Georgian houses, Rolle Chapel is in the background

Rolle Chapel from East Terrace. Built in 1813 and demolished in 1893 after being replaced by St Peter's Church

sheds. Back in Chapel Street, the house next to the brook was a private dwelling, except for a short time when it became a fish-and-chip shop.

This about completes our walk of the main streets of the town. If we now go on to the junction of Fore Street Hill and East Terrace you will see an imposing block of red-brick houses with bay windows, Nos 1 to 5 East Terrace. These houses, like all the others in East Terrace, have gardens across the road, an unusual feature in the town. And, as with West Terrace, the houses are on one side of the road only, facing south, in a favoured position, where glimpses of the sea can be seen, especially from the upper windows. Beyond these houses, as we walk westward, were three large houses, all of which have been replaced by modern ones. But the rest of the terrace as far as Chapel Hill is more or less as I knew it when I was young. One thing I must mention here, on Chapel Hill was the old parish church, Rolle Chapel, built in 1813 and replaced just before the turn of the century, by St Peter's,

View of the houses on West Terrace and Upper West Terrace, with Ingleside House on the left and Dial House on the right, on top of the hill

Conservatory at Ingleside House

the new parish church. I am told that the gates across East Terrace used to be locked except when services were being conducted and you had to walk all around through the town to get to the other side. The half circular shapes of the Chapel forecourts were 'coffin turners'; they are still visible in the design of the road and gardens in East Terrace. When hearses were drawn by horses it was no easy matter to turn around.

Proceeding towards West Terrace, Chapel Hill on the right splits in two. The left-hand side leads to Upper West Terrace where Ingleside House was at the far end. It was one of the most imposing houses of the old town, with a remarkable conservatory which should never have been destroyed. There used to be '*thés dansants*' and other pleasurable activities held there. But all that is gone and with it an era that seems but a far memory now. The right-hand side leads to Dial House and the old cricket field where sports and other activities used to be held. If you go further still, you reach the Games Club on the left and the Bowls and Lawn Tennis Club on the right. Just past the pavilion is Kersbrook Reservoir; but in my time it was known to the locals as 'The Crab Pot', because of its shape.

Back to West Terrace, some of the houses are new, and others have seen drastic external alterations. In one of the original houses my uncle

George Searle used to be groom and gardener to Dr Tom Evans, father of the Dr Tom Evans who is still remembered by many of the older people of the town. The road runs level to a blind end where The Lawn, a large house, latterly owned by Mr J.W. Palmer stood. The grounds used to extend right down to Station Road. This area has also given way to 'progress'. Where St Peter's Parish Church and its grounds are now, used to be a grazing field owned by Mr Tom Hitt of Chapel Street. As you turn towards the High Street the houses on your right are also entirely new; the end one now being the health centre. They were built in the grounds of a large boarding-house belonging to people called Watkins.

We will now take the short walk around the post office to Station Road, where again there has been so much rebuilding as to make the place quite unrecognizable. Moor Lane, once no more than a country lane, started right at the High Street. It was only when the railway line was built at around the turn of the century that the lane was widened, and turned into a road which was then

The Lawn

The large house that replaced The Lawn, photographed from the field where St Peter's Church now stands

The house on the corner of Moor Lane – it was presumably demolished when the road was widened

Salterton Station and Signal Box

renamed Station Road; the higher part further along being Station Hill. Next to the brook, which is still open at this point, was a stable for three horses and some carts. These stables were used by a haulage firm whose main customer was the local council. The horses' manure was stacked just inside the yard, right next to the road, but no one seemed to mind. This was done at a good number of such places and was taken for granted. Next came a two-storey stabling, called Scaddings Stables, with lofts up over. It faced into a large yard at right angles to Station Road, and besides stables for several horses, there was ample room for carriages and other equipment used to run a mews with carriages etc. for hire. Opposite were two decrepit-looking cottages whose only outlook was the stables, with the accompanying smell and activity. They were often invaded by rats and rather blocked of light, as a forage store abutted immediately out from one of them. There was yet another yard next to this where two horses were kept, and vehicles for the delivery of goods, heavy and light, from the station goods yard to every part of the town and surrounding area. Later, these premises were used by Colonel Chichester, owner of Ingleside House. He didn't use them as stabling but as a garage for one of the ever-increasing number of motor cars in the town; the adjoining cottage was for the use of his gardener. There were two other cottages built at half right-angles to Station Road, and next to them, at a similar angle, came a large pair of double doors which led to the grounds of The Lawn, too high to allow a look at the grounds. A very high wall ran from them along the road to Gospel Hall, which is now exactly the same as when I attended Sunday school there.

On the other side of the road, at the beginning of Station Road, was a large house called Archbrook, the whole corner of which collapsed during a storm. Next to it was another stable and coach-house, which has since been converted to living accommodation. Then comes the brook, alongside which runs a roadway to Oaklodge, at one time a private school. Around the corner were the back entrances to a pair of semi-detached houses, later converted into council offices. During the Second World War they housed two large families evacuated from London. Further along this roadway, at the back, were more cow

Station Road viewed from the Gospel Hall. Gush's Field is on the left

sheds where Mr P. Gush kept his herd of dairy cows. These used to be driven along Station Road to Gush's Field, opposite the Gospel Hall. The two shops next to the brook in Station Road were built in the garden of the first of the semi-detached houses, where in my young days a retired doctor of the name of Deas lived. At the side of the second house was an orchard which stretched to Gush's Field. The pavement ended at the beginning of the orchard and there was always running water in the gutter, presumably from the marshy part of the field. At the rear of the field, on a higher level, was Mr Gush's market garden and meadows for the grazing of his cows. The site of the orchard has seen a lot of development, including the new fire station, the Public Hall and the Church Institute, since demolished and replaced by modern dwellings.

The houses in Station Road facing the field were mostly private residences, but some were rather high-class apartment houses. Beyond them, at the beginning of Station Hill, was a high brick wall behind which was a field that went back as far as Westfield Close. Then came Bickley's slaughterhouse with more fields at the rear. Still behind the wall there is Shandford, now an old people's home. It used to belong to Lady Alice Ewing, who had been lady-in-waiting to Lady Rolle at Bicton House. The two or three houses on the other side, next to the railway station, were built in the early 1900s, as was the majority of Clinton Terrace.

We will now retrace our steps to Rolle Square. Rolle Road, the road connecting the High Street to the cliff path, has seen little change. The two small fishermen's cottages opposite the Rolle Hotel were turned into shops and a café. My sister Elsie used to live in one of the cottages, and the living room-cum-kitchen was known to me as 'Stickle Annie's Kitchen', why, I couldn't tell. The other was lived in by one of the Sedgemore fishing family, and the story went round that one day Mr Sedgemore came home, cold and wet, went to the teapot and found no tea in it, so threw the pot out of the window. He went to get some bread and butter and the butter wouldn't spread, so he trod it into the coconut mat. The life of the fishermen could be hard, but I think that in many cases the life of their wives was even harder.

At the end of the road now are public toilets, for which a corner of the garden of No 1 Cliff Terrace was used. The very first public convenience, a single toilet for ladies, was to be found on the cliff path at the rear of the Coffee Tavern. A more elaborate affair was put up later, to the left of the Rolle Hotel, behind Perriam's. This was replaced by a building under the cliff path adjoining the mortuary, where, during the First World War, bodies washed up from the sea were kept for identification. We boys used to peer through the keyholes to get a glimpse of the dead bodies inside. A very special toilet, but not for public use, was to be found at the end of the cul-de-sac off South Parade, in the yard where the bathing machines were stored. Lady Rolle used to drive into Budleigh Salterton during the summer months, attended by her lady's maid, and the Rolle Estate built this toilet specially for her convenience.

Cliff Terrace which connects Rolle Road and Cliff Road, used to be a very quiet road before the coming of the motor car and short-term parking. There are houses on one side only of the Terrace, facing south. Some of the houses in this favoured position have been replaced by modern ones. Originally, all were private family residences, but between the wars, when the town was a sought-after watering-place, more than half of them were used as apartment houses. The gardens opposite on the seaward side extending to the cliff path did not belong to the houses in Cliff Terrace; they were rented from

the Rolle Estate, and anyone could apply to have a garden there on a short lease. Many had a summer-house erected near the cliff path, from which a lovely view of the bay can be seen. One of these summer-houses used to be the venue for an annual harvest supper for the fishermen. It was given by two sisters, the Misses Goullet, as a thanksgiving for the harvest of the sea, which in those times was a considerable help to the prosperity of the town.

All the houses on the Terrace had a rear entrance in Queen Street. The original gardens to the houses were on this side, facing north. But there were always various sheds and outhouses to be found in them. Because of this situation there were only four small cottages, still there, on this side of Queen Street, near the Rolle end. On the High Street side were back entrances to the shops, or outhouses belonging to them, including a slaughterhouse, a bakehouse and a fishmonger's yard – all with the accompanying smells. Near the Cliff Road end, a lot of room was taken up by the old Church School, built in 1842 and moved to the new premises in Moor Lane in 1912. Next to the school was a cul-de-sac, at right angles to Queen Street, in which were four small cottages. In 1823 the front room of one of them became the first Lodge Room of the local Freemasons – when only a few larger towns had such a meeting place.

The lower part of Cliff Road has altered quite a lot. The whole of the road from Queen Street to the building behind Creedy's was taken up by a row of small terraced houses with tiny front gardens. The end one was double-fronted, and occupied by a chimney sweep. He owned one of the donkeys of the town and he stabled it at the back of the house. This house collapsed during a winter storm, but, as in the case of the other houses mentioned that had suffered the same fate, nobody was seriously injured. The small cottages were lived in by large families, and it was said that there were so many boys in the road, you could form three soccer teams with them. The small building behind Creedy's has been used for many different purposes, among the first being a garage to house small motor coaches. I say small because by modern standards they were truly small. They were owned by Albert Searle, whose father in earlier days owned the station bus and ran a carrier's business between

Fisherman's Cottage, turned into a café

Looking into Queen Street from Cliff Road, with the old church school on the left

Cliff Road with Feather's Longroom and the old cottages opposite. In the background, St Peter's church is being built. Above is one of the old houses in West Terrace

The original Rosemullion Hotel with Cliff House on the right

the railway station and all parts of the town. On the opposite side of the road was the Feathers Long Room, and higher up, more small cottages. The row ended with a larger double-fronted house known as Cliff Cottage, which in my time was always an apartment house. Next came The Cliff, still there, a gentleman's residence of character. Until 1910 it was lived in by Dr Brushfield, a 'vurriner' (foreigner) to Devon, but soon accepted on account of his interest in the community. He built an annexe for his library of over 10 000 books and manuscripts, for which he employed local craftsmen, members of the Cowd and Keslake families. I understand that it has a beautiful ceiling and delicately patterned fireplace. The Gothic windows with coloured glass give it the look of a chapel. At the top of the road is the Rosemullion Hotel; it too was originally a private house, consisting only of the central section with the five gables, but enlarged at different times to accommodate the ever-increasing number of guests.

All the roads westward of Cliff Road were cul-de-sacs for vehicles, but for pedestrians there was mostly a path leading up to Jubilee Plantation, Hackley Field and, further west, the golf links. They lead off at right angles from West Hill, which continues from the High Street in a straight run. When I first knew Jubilee Plantation, a small wood planted with conifers to commemorate the Golden Jubilee of Queen Victoria. it was well laid out with footpaths and seats, but when I last saw it, it had been allowed to revert almost to nature.

Victoria Place, only a lane in my time and not much more today, had a row of red-brick houses on the left following the incline of the hill, and small cottages on the opposite side. There was little scope for alteration, and it remains a part of the old town. At the top end were larger houses enjoying a fine view over the bay and over the hills inland. The last house on the right was Montpellier, at one time a girls's boarding school and later on converted into a hotel. The area to the west, now built up quite a lot, was largely fields in my young days with just a few houses here and there. There were houses at the bottom of the hill, along West Hill Road, mostly private residences, the first ones built in the 1870s. Past Victoria Place, the Masonic Hall, still there, was built in 1891. Next to it was the Public Rooms, opened in 1861 and, as the name suggests, used

Looking down Victoria Place as it was early in the century, with Archbrook House on the other side of West Hill

Looking down West Hill. The Public Rooms are on the right

for public events. After the Public Hall in Station Road had been built in 1926, the old building was used for various purposes, latterly by J.W. Palmer as a furniture repository and eventually demolished during the Second World War when it was hit by a bomb.

Westbourne Terrace

Thatched cottages at the lower end of Fountain Hill

Westbourne Terrace, further along West Hill, had a row of imposing semi-detached houses on the right and a wicket gate at the top to give access to Jubilee Plantation. On the other side were three meadows reaching down to the Public Rooms. Fountain Hill, the next cul-de-sac, was named, no doubt, from the drinking-fountain at the bottom of the hill. It was placed there for horses and cattle to drink, and it had a lower trough for dogs. Near the fountain were some lovely thatched cottages, demolished, if I remember correctly, in about 1926 or 1927. North View Road, leading off Fountain Hill, ended, in my time, at the house known as Pine Hollow.

Further along West Hill used to be old cottages, all demolished except Edgehill, a superior kind of boarding-house when I knew it first. The mentioning of Edgehill reminds me of another old character of early days, a lady known as Miss Lobb, an eccentric person who used to embarrass people by asking them if they could tell her the time. As very few people possessed a watch, they would say they couldn't, where upon she would produce, from the large basket she always carried, an alarm clock, and say, 'Now, please, will you tell me the time?' People would cross the road, or even turn back to avoid her. Next came White's Nurseries, an old-established family business, run first by White senior and then for many years by this two sons. Castle Cottage and Hollybank, two old houses, take us to the bottom of Sherbrook Hill. This road was known in my time as Smart's Hill because of a farm of that name in the area, leased from the Rolle Estate.

Almost opposite Sherbrook Hill is Halse Hill, with two old cottages, still there. At the bottom of the hill the road fords the brook which runs through the town. On the west side of Halse Hill is Little Common, rather more cultivated than when I first knew it. On the otherside of West Hill was a large house, The Firs, first a private house, then a hotel and now an old people's home. Next came a rambling type of bungalow, Woodlands, which had a gazebo-like structure over a well in front. I am told it was formerly almshouses, built to commemorate Queen Victoria's Golden Jubilee. The bungalow has gone, together with gazebo, well and all, and in place of it and its

Woodlands, now replaced by a housing estate

BS-F

77

extensive parklands, is now a whole new estate of twenty-four houses – another sign of the changing times.

West Hill ends at Links Road, which then consisted of just a few houses at the bottom of the road, built by 'Little Fred' Cowd at the turn of the century. As the name shows, Links Road leads to the golf links with its fine clubhouse. The higher parts of the golf course afford an unrivalled view over the bay and its hinterland. The area used to be common land, very colourful with heather and

The Clubhouse early this century

gorse. I am informed, that according to the law as it was then, anyone spending money on common land could thereafter claim it as their own, and as the Rolle Estate had money to spend and actually did so, the land could be claimed by them. What exactly was done to it, I couldn't tell, but at the turn of the century there was a Budleigh Golf Club which became, in 1902, the East Devon Golf Club, which it still is. The club has always been a proprietary one; earlier it belonged to Lord Clinton and is now leased from the Clinton Devon Estate. There was a gentlemen's course with eighteen holes, and a ladies' course with nine holes. I have already mentioned that I used to caddy for Mr Hughes of Cintra. Caddying gave many a Salterton lad the opportunity to earn some money, for you were paid either a shilling or sixpence for a round, and on a fine summer's day you could do three rounds – which meant a lot of walking.

Continuing along the Exmouth Road the only houses in my youth were two low thatched semi-detached houses on the right, still there, fronted by a wall of flint stones. The unsuspecting

Looking towards Exmouth from the highest point of the golf course

caller would be greeted by the loud barking of 'a thousand and one dalmations' emerging at every window. On the left, about half-way to Landsdowne Road, there was a small farmhouse and outbuildings, roughly where Moorlands Road starts. Lansdowne Road consisted of six large houses, and then dwindled to a narrow road and a footpath leading to the golf-links and the cliff path, Sandy Bay and Exmouth. Almost opposite this road, at the junction of Knowle Village Road, is a small triangle where there used to be an AA box, manned in daylight hours by an AA scout who was always at hand to give advice and assistance, a very necessary service in the early days of motoring, and most welcome at the bottom of Knowle Hill. The triangle of grass around the box was always kept spick and span, with flower beds an added attraction.

As we walk towards Knowle Village, Lee Ford House is on our left, built for Gilbert Cowd in about 1800. It then consisted only of the section with the Regency look. It did not stay long in the family as the son died without leaving children. The estate was eventually sold and a charitable

AA scout, Bert Pollard with Perce Watkins, the first Post Office van driver in front of the Triangle at the bottom of Knowle Hill

trust set up, administered by East Budleigh Parish Church, for the benefit of poor people.

Very little is left of the old Knowle Village, or 'Big Knowle', as it was called in my time. The

Knowle Village with cob cottages and brick-built Rolle Cottages with pantile roofs

road running through it divides the village in two, half belonging to St Thomas, Exeter, the other half to Salterton. The old village consisted of a few cob cottages with thatched roofs and front doors opening right on to the road, a block of red-brick houses known then as Rolle Cottages, a forge, a small school and the Britannia Inn. The original inn was a low thatched building, always referred to as the Dog and Donkey. It was run by Mr and Mrs Doney, who also ran a business distributing sacks of coal. During the war, when Mr Doney, like many other men of the town was away, Mrs Doney carried on the business and delivered the coal herself, carrying the sacks on her shoulder.

Dalditch Lane, flanked by the brook that runs through Budleigh Salterton, is much the same as when I first walked it in my early youth. I mention it because we pass under one of the highest railway bridges I have ever seen, carrying the old railway line far above the road on a very high embankment. We always called it Million Bridge,

probably because that number of bricks were used in its construction. Nearby is Dalditch Farm, and a large house I remember being built for a reputed millionaire. At the time, it was talked about a lot as it was constructed of cob in the old-fashioned way, and known to us as Cob House. It also had a thatched roof, unusual material then as it had not been used very much for many years owing to the fire risk. The name of the house was later changed to Long Orchard.

Knowle Road, a long narrow lane, takes us right back to Little Knowle and West Hill. It is flanked by numerous houses now, but in my time there were few landmarks. On the left was a farmhouse, Lower Knowle Farm, which was destroyed by fire many years ago and never rebuilt, and further along a sand quarry, now a nursery. Near the junction with Halse Hill and Dark Lane we pass Clysthayes Farm on the left and, on the right, Burnside, a cottage which was the home of the district nurse in my time. Further on, where the road takes a sharp turn to the

The Britannia Inn in Knowle Village locally known as the 'Dog & Donkey'. The road leads out of Knowle Village on the way to East Budleigh

80

right, you will find on the left-hand side Park Lane, a cul-de-sac leading to Park Lodge and Park House, which was a private school for boys run by Mr and Mrs Martinua. On the other side of the lane, now fully developed with new housing, were meadows where animals used to graze. Knowle Road wanders on, with little change, past Lilybrook on the right, behind a stone wall and

Knowle Road with Watt's Farm, Clysthayes (still there), and Bickley's House in the distance

Park House when it was a private school

hidden by tall trees, and two houses on the left that faced a meadow bordered by the brook at the far end. Then we go over the brook and past Little Knowle House and some other old houses and cottages, all on the right, the Baptist church, Ebenezer Chapel, built in 1844, among them. On the left, behind a stone wall topped by pebbles from the beach, are the grounds of a nursery, and beyond, a house called Willowmead. The road then comes out in West Hill, near the vicarage.

Dark Lane, which we pased on our left, must have got is name because of the high banks on either side with large trees on top over-shadowing the lane. It was also referred to as Smuggler's Lane, Tunnel Lane or Cow Lane. The banks are of a soft sandstone which has eroded since my young days exposing the roots of the trees. At dusk, bats used to fly about the lane from hidden roosts in crevices or small caves. The area at the far end of the lane was nearly all fields in my early days. There was Tidwell House or Tidwell Barton on the road to East Budleigh, a large Georgian house with farm buildings. It is widely thought that it took its name from a well in the field opposite, the water of which rises and

Dark Lane

Looking towards Little Knowle with the pebble topped stone wall on the right

82

falls according to the level of the tide at sea, and which was never known to run dry, even in the driest of summers. But I am told that the original name was Todvill, the 'vill' or residence of Tod. It was eventually bought by Lord Rolle for the manager of his estate. In my time the house was said to be haunted, but there was never anything to substantiate the story. Nearby is a wicket gate leading through fields to Shortwood, where in spring we would go to pick wild primroses, which were to be found in abundance. On Shortwood Common, villagers from the surrounding countryside used to cut the plentiful ferns as bedding for their animals, and turf, which was of a fine quality, for making lawns.

At the junction of Greenway Lane and Barn Lane, just country lanes in my time, was an embankment spanned by a railway bridge, and in one of the nearby fields my father ran a small-holding where he kept a few pigs and grew quite a lot of produce which he sold locally. In Bedlands Lane was a small estate of cottages known as Frewins, built in the 1910s, for Lady Mathieson, who lived in Otterbourne House in Coastguard Road. The houses were constructed to her design and were fitted very sparsely and frugally even for those times. No plastered walls or ceilings, the doors of the ledge-and-strap design, with stable latches and bolts for fastening them. There were small gardens back and front, and with them went a nearby allotment. Lady Mathieson imposed certain conditions for the letting of the houses: the rent was to be no more than 2s. 6d. a week, and the applicant must already be living in the district. Much later I visited a Quaker housing estate at Jordans in Buckinghamshire, and although the houses were of much larger dimension they struck me by their similarity. I have wondered ever since if the design of Frewins could have been influenced by that cult. But I have since heard that Lady Mathieson lost money in Germany during the inflation after the First World War, and that this accounted for the way in which the houses were finished.

In Moor Lane the only houses in my youth were four cottages which lay well back from the road, at right-angles to the lane. To get to them you had to walk past Frank Watt's stables, a very substantial wooden building which used to house his horses, carts, and later, Foden steam

Frewins

Jocelyn Road when newly built

wagons. Cottages and stables have long since been demolished and an attractive council estate occupies the site. It was expanded at various times and now extends as far as Barn Lane and Bedlands. Greenway Lane, too, was a country road in my youth, all fields, with the exception of a row of houses near Jocelyn Road. The stationmaster's cottage was the only house in Leas Road across the railway bridge, and there were houses in Copplestone Road, but the row was only completed after the First World War. Jocelyn Road was the first road to be developed in the area, and a three-bedroomed terrace house could be bought for as little as £180. True, they were not very sumptuous, having small rooms, no hot-water system or indoor lavatory, just a cold-water tap in the scullery, a sink not more than six inches deep, and a brick built-in copper for heating the water on washing day. At that price they were bought quickly but there were no mortgages, as we know them today. It was in one of these houses that I started married life, renting accommodation until we had saved enough money to buy Whitemoor, near Granary Lane.

When Jocelyn Road was completed there was a lull for a good many years; the fields on this side of Greenway more or less derelict, a playground for children. When building restarted, well after the war, the infilling of this area was very rapid. A familiar sight was what became known as Carter's Train: a traction engine towing three trailers loaded with half bricks or brick boxes which were used in the building of the dividing walls of the terrace houses. The critics, and there were many, thought the houses would not last, but they are still standing today. Carters must have cleared the two brickyards at Exmouth of an accumulation of broken bricks that had been gathering for a good many years.

Copp Hill Lane, originally part of Greenway Lane, was developed later. Before, there were fields and allotments, only one of which remains. One of the fields was tended by 'Curly' Sedgemore, and the story goes that on a stormy afternoon, when there was little prospect of him being able to do anything useful at the beach, he and his wife decided to go to Copp Hill and erect a duck-house which they had had delivered. Taking what tools he thought necessary for the job, they set off up Chapel Street, over the wooden railway bridge and then on to the field. After attending to the livestock, which always expected attention on their arrival, they then started erecting the duck-house. All went well until they came to hang the door, when they discovered they had not included a screwdriver with the tools. 'Curly' was very upset, and started to 'romance' in his particular way. Although I or anybody else, for that matter, never heard him actually swear, the words he used might have had the same meaning. Jemima tried to smooth matters by offering to go home and fetch one. Although having doubts as to whether she knew what tool was needed, he agreed and as she set off, proceeded to do a few jobs to pass the time. He dug two bags of 'teddies' (potatoes), picked a few vegetables and

cleared out the poultry houses, by which time it was getting on towards dark. So he set off for home, assuming that she had either failed to find a screwdriver or had met a friend. He got back as far as Fulton's or Dial House at the top of Chapel Street Hill. To use his own words. 'T'was nearly dark, but I zeed 'ur, puffing like a grampus', (which was not surprizing, as she had come up a steep hill in a hurry). I zade to 'ur, "Wurr evee bin, Jemima?", and 'ur zade, "Aw weel, I cooden vind un anywhere. I 'ope thickee 'ul do". And 'ur 'olds up a vulltee gurt jack-plane!'

Near the foot-bridge Copp Hill Lane turns sharply to the left, and at the end of the lane we come to a steep hill dropping down into Kersbrook Valley. At one time, in early motoring days, it was used for motor car trials. If the car could get to the top without the engine stalling it was considered to be good. But a lot failed almost at the top, where a sharp bend proved too much.

At the bottom this steep lane runs through the farmyard of Kersbrook Farm into Kersbrook Lane, still a narrow country lane, which links the two roads running from either end of Budleigh Salterton to East Budleigh. About halfway along you will find a small red-brick cottage called Pennypark perched on a bank at the side of the lane. Nearby on the brook side is the pumping station that sends the water from Tidwell to the three reservoirs of the town, miles from here, one as far away as West Down Beacon on the very top of the cliffs. This station was built on the site of the old Kersbrook Mill, which had a huge water-wheel. Following the direction of the brook, we wander through the village with its old cottages and eventually join the main road to East Budleigh. Kersbrook Lane now turns left up to the road, but that was not so in my time. Then the road, very much narrower, dropped in a bend to the level of the brook where it joined the lane. In doing so, East Budleigh Road ran under another tall railway bridge of unusual architecture, a true work of art: an arch built of bricks diagonal to the road. We can still go and admire it by following the footpath that leads from Kersbrook Lane to the main road at the junction with Granary Lane, walking the old road. Now, all we have to do to complete our 'Walk about the Town', is to follow East Budleigh Road, and it will bring us past Stoneborough to the Cottage Hospital, where we started.

Kersbrook Cottage as seen from Copp Hill with the train approaching the railway bridge

COMMUNITY LIFE

ENTERTAINMENT

Although Poplar Row was a little back street, we did not miss a lot of the activities going on. In those days there was no television, no wireless, and the gramophone was, more or less, in its infancy. Imagine what a treat it was when the German bands, who used to visit most towns and villages, came, playing selections of music. There were other street musicians performing in the road, although the few coppers they collected must have been hardly worth their while. Another regular feature of the road scene was the travelling bazaars, men pushing or pulling small vehicles loaded with household items. They were known as sixpenny bazaars and they never failed to give the Row a visit. Then there was, besides the daily newspapers, the weekly papers. One of them, called the *Exmouth Chronicle*, was sold along the streets by an old man ringing a bell. He would call out the headlines, going through the main items so well that you would almost know all there was in the paper, without buying it. The *Express and Echo* besides being sold at the newsagents, was sold by Jimmy Harland, a crippled hunchback on crutches who, after making a stand at the street corner, would then walk, in all weathers, around the outer town to regular customers, and all for the price of a penny. The Sunday newspapers were sold for twopence by Mr Tom Pearcey on a three-wheeled barrow in a similar manner.

Off the High Street in Cliff Road, at the rear of the Feathers Hotel, was a recreation room known as the Feathers Long Room. As the name suggests, it was a long room, perhaps out of proportion to its width, and it was used for small public meetings, including Anglican and other church services, committee meetings, and what used to be known then as 'smoking concerts'. At these concerts the locals would get together for a sing-song. No set programme was arranged and anybody who felt bold enough to stand in front of the audience – there was no stage – could take part. After a time, when the drinks began to take effect, one could hear all manner of songs, recitations etc., some good, some perhaps a little ribald. There was no bar in the room, but drinks were allowed to be brought up from the Feathers below. This room was over the stabling in the yard, which was a coaching station, and there was always a distinctive smell about. The place was hit by a bomb during the Second World War, and that was the end of it.

The Masonic Hall, at the start of West Hill, was at one time a cinema run by a local tradesman, not, I think, for a great financial gain but rather for the good of the town in general and for the younger generation in particular. Prices, as far as I remember, were from 9d. to 1s. 6d., and if you wanted to sit in the raised plush tip-up seats at the rear you had to pay extra. On Saturday afternoons children were admitted for 1d. The cinema ran for a good number of years in the Masonic Hall, from about 1912 to 1918. After the war some film shows were held in the Drill Hall in Moor Lane, and later still in the Public Hall in Station Road – until the coming of television caused audiences gradually to dwindle to nothing.

The Public Rooms a little further along West Hill towards Westbourne Terrace was a larger entertainment hall. There, various professional shows would be held, as well as amateur plays and concerts, lectures and dances. Meetings of various societies took place, and the Literary Institute had its reading room and library there. It was an important centre for public life. A show which used to come regularly was Doctor Barnado's Boys, who would entertain for over an

hour, and a notable feature was the ringing of handbells, which usually brought the house down. Admission charges were small, they had to be in those days. I remember children were admitted for 2d. In later years, when the Public Hall in Station Road came into being, there was less demand for these places. The Masonic Hall is still used, but nothing near as much, and it would have no doubt disappeared like the Public Rooms, but for the fact of its principal use.

A very important annual event was the Carnival which took place in October often late in the month, and was held in aid of local charities. A great many people took part in it, not only on the actual day or days, but in the months of meetings and the preparations which led up to the event. Anything that could raise money would be

Carnival scene in Marine Parade. The donkey 'borrowed' for the event was painted like a zebra, but it unfortunately died from the effects, to the great consternation of those who played the prank

Carnival capers in Station Road. The town crier, Archie Teed with bear and clowns and a barrel organ. Notice the beautiful wall, now demolished to make room for the shops next to the brook

considered, such as stalls in the streets to sell food and other goods, mainly gifts from various patrons, a fair, not unlike those of today but made up of such things as 'hoop-la' or 'shove halfpenny' and simple little side-shows for which a small admission charge would be made. I remember two such shows: one was the 'Swimming Match'; someone in fancy dress would be on a platform beating a drum and calling attention, and when you got inside all you saw was a single match floating in a bowl of water; in the other it was announced that by paying a small fee you could see the largest water otter ever seen. What you actually saw was a tremendous kettle. Things like that would be considered 'simple' today, but they went down very well in the early part of the century. But the main attraction was the torch-light procession, which would assemble in Coast-guard Road soon after dark. I know similar events are held today, but to anybody of my generation there is not the same atmosphere about them, as they are now nearly always held in daylight hours.

Remember there was no electricity then in Budleigh Salterton, and all the tableaux, bands, etc., had to be illuminated by flaming torches with naked flames kept alight by wax and oil. They gave off a distinctive smell and lots of smoke, and the bearers were black by the time the event was over. The tableaux were, then as now, mounted on farm wagons or tradesmen's vehicles loaned for the event, but of course were all drawn by horses. A fine sight they made, specially groomed, manes and tails traced (plaited) and be-ribboned, and the leather and brasses of their harnesses gleaming like new. They took a lot of controlling, as the noise of the bands and the cheering of the crowds were sounds unusual to them. The procession would be made up of some fifty or so items, led by the Marshall chosen for the occasion and the local band. Other bands from Exmouth, East Budleigh, Newton Poppleford, Tipton St John etc. would be placed at intervals in the procession, for even small villages used to have their own bands in those days.

Budleigh Salterton Town Band. Their smart new uniforms cost 15s. each

There were footmen in fancy costumes interspersed, and mounted men and groups of dancers or cyclists with decorated cycles. The tableaux would represent almost anything; from famous characters out of well-known scenes from operas, fairy tales, nursery rhymes, history or mythology, whether it be Sleeping Beauty, The Three Graces, Templars, Mikado and Geisha, or Joan of Arc, each in a particular setting. More homely scenes were also represented, such as an 'Old English Lady', 'Working Bakery', 'Village Blacksmith', 'Barber's Shop', 'Fortune Teller', etc.

I especially remember two very fine tableaux, one entitled 'If those lips could only speak', representing a famous oil portrait of a lady (I think it was by Gainsborough). It was a simple idea, and was done by having a lady sitting, dressed the same as the lady in the oil painting, inside a very large carved gilt frame. The other was titled 'Britannia'; again a simple idea and easy to make, just a large hoop with the words 'One Penny'

suspended from the top of the circle and a lady placed in it, dressed as Britannia and holding a trident in her hand.

My very earliest memory of a carnival – it was in 1907 when I was only three years old – was being lifted down, very sleepy, off the wagon by my father and being carried up Pebble Lane to Poplar Row after having taken part in a tableau called 'The Old Woman Who Lived In A Shoe'.

The procession would set off in Coastguard Road, thence along The Parade, Fore Street, High Street, Station Road, then back again up West Hill to the bottom of the Golf Links Road, turn down West Hill, up by the Post Office to West and East Terraces, up Fore Street Hill, Coastguard Road, The Parade, Fore Street to the Rolle Hotel, where the massed bands would play 'God Save the King'.

These processions were preceded and followed by other events, such as musical drills and maypole dances held in the Masonic Hall or

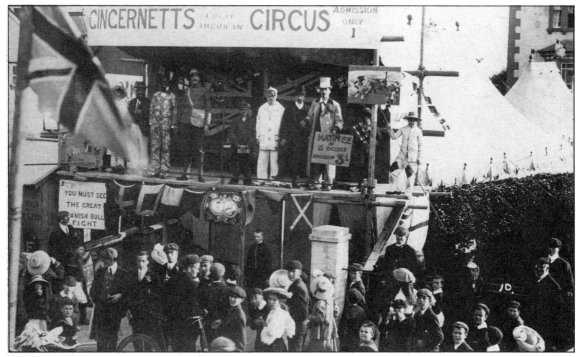

Circus in Rolle Square with sideshows organized to raise money for charity

Public Rooms; shooting galleries where you could have three shots for a penny; magic shows and other attractions for a penny where 'people who take life too seriously' were not admitted; circuses in marquees in Rolle Square; tents where you could have your fortune told, and, as a grand finale, a fancy dress ball at the Public Rooms which would last well into the morning. The carnivals were suspended during the war years and, although taken up again after the First World War, they never seem to have quite regained their former magic and excitement which my generation remembers with pure nostalgia.

Sports days and gymkhanas were also annual events (although the gymkhanas had nothing to do with horses). They too were in aid of charities or sports clubs, and in the early days used to be held in the old cricket field on top of the hill backing on to the town, an ideal place for such events. That site was also the home of the local football club, the 'Robins', long since removed to Page's Field at the corner of Greenway Lane and Barn Lane. Then there was a swimming club with its headquarters on the beach, where, weather permitting, swimming galas and water polo matches were held, again with the purpose of fund-raising. Swimming races made up the main events, but what aroused the greatest interest and amusement was a water polo match and a punt chase. For the water polo match, which was played against a prominent visiting team, goal-posts and nets were moored, and a pitch marked out with ropes and corks. For the punt chase, two swimmers were provided with a small rowing-boat each, the object being for one to catch the other. The boats were positioned at a given distance apart and the game was started by firing a pistol. The man chasing the fugitive was given a period of time to catch him, the time being divided into three parts; for the first part they had to stay in the boat, for the second, in the water, and the last episode took place on the beach. These galas did not last for long, as, owing to the open nature of the bay, what started as a fine morning with a smooth sea often turned into a stormy day with the sea too rough to hold the events.

In the 1920s there were regular concert parties held during the summer months below the Saltings Hill, by the Denton Concert Party. This

Budleigh Salterton Swimming Club

Watching the swimming gala from the beach

consisted of orchestra, chorus, 'pom-poms gay are we', and juggling acts, with the audience taking part where appropriate. The concerts took place in an open marquee with only the stage covered, and the children, who would sit on the cliff nearby, had a free show.

During my time, a St John's Ambulance Brigade was started, of which I became a member. It began with a house-to-house collection to raise money for uniforms and other necessary equipment. The Brigade attended any function if requested, including sports events and football matches. In the summer months there was a First Aid Post opposite the beach at The Parade, to assist in minor accidents and even with such matters as sunburn. There was also the Coast Life-Saving Brigade with a crew of about twenty. They had a boat-house (now the café close the shelter on the beach) which contained two boats used by the guards for boat-drill. The boats were never intended, as was often supposed, for life-saving purposes, although the place was often referred to as 'The Lifeboat House'. The object of this Brigade was to save life in the event of a shipwreck, with the help of rocket apparatus. I am pleased to say that during the time I served as No 14 we had little cause to use it. But there were four practice calls a year which attracted a great number of spectators. A maroon would be fired to summon the crew, who had to leave anything they were doing and report to the Coastguard Station. We would take the wagon holding all the gear to the mouth of the River Otter where a few members of the crew would be put ashore on the other side of the river and act as passengers and crew of the stricken vessel. A high post on the cliff across the river represented the mast of the ship, at which a large rocket would be fired with a light rope attached to it, If successful, as it usually was, a thick hawser was then attached to the rope and it was hauled 'aboard' and the hawser made fast to the highest part of the mast. A large triangle was then erected at the shore end with a pulley at the centre through which the shore end of the hawser was passed and secured to the ground by a very large anchor. The breeches-buoy was then hauled out to the 'ship' and the crew were hauled ashore, one-by-one, and treated for shock or other troubles. My duty as No 14 was to restore the line that was attached to the rocket; a very

important matter as it must run out at a terrific speed without fouling. Usually when the 'victim' was brought ashore there would be a demonstration of the Schafer Method for restoring anyone apparently drowned, a duty which usually also came my way.

Another regular feature of life in the town were the fairs with merry-go-rounds, coconut-shies, skittles, and shows of various types. At a time when there was little other entertainment to be had, they were well attended. When a circus visited the town the boys used to get up early to help erect the tents, for which they were rewarded with a free ticket, much appreciated, as many of them couldn't have afforded the sixpence required to buy one. The fairs and circuses moved from site to site over the years; from Webber's Field in Coastguard Road to Leas Road, Moor Lane, Greenway Lane etc., as these sites were gradually built on.

Then there were the special events connected with the Royal Family. Nowadays people sit in front of the T.V. and watch what is going on, which is all very well but it does not create the festive atmosphere that was typical of such events in my time. I remember the coronation of King George V in June 1911. A service was held in Rolle Square followed by parties in the streets, where tables and benches were set up and people sat down for a meal. On the occasion of the Silver Jubilee of King George and Queen Mary on the 6 May 1935, there was, in the morning, a procession of the public bodies through the town, followed by a thanksgiving service in the open. In the afternoon there was a childrens' fancy dress procession, followed by tea for them. Athletic sports events were held at various places, and the local bands contributed in their own way. In the evening there was dancing in the Public Hall, and at 10 p.m., a bonfire in Hackley Field. And then there was Empire Day, of which I have fond memories because it meant no school. The children assembled in the morning in the playground, where patriotic songs were sung, followed by sports; the rest of the day was free.

In my time there was, of course, always a big social gap between what we used to call 'them' and 'us'. That is to say the people who lived in the large houses and had servants, and the locals who earned their living as farmers, tradesmen, fishermen, etc., or by running establishments for

The Coronation of George V and Queen Mary. A service was held in Rolle Square

Local band playing in Knowle Village for the Silver Jubilee of King George V, 5th May 1935. Wallace Pope (trumpet), Walter Bedford (violin), Ted Prew (drums), Ernie Payne (saxophone) and Clarice Kemp (piano). The old Knowle Village school is in the background

Starting off celebrations on Empire Day with a trumpet call and rifle volley

visitors. Many of 'them' were retired colonial officials or army officers. I have already mentioned that my sisters, upon reaching the age of twelve, would go into service at one of the big houses, and how I used to go cleaning shoes and knives as a lad, or caddy for the gentleman of the house. Many a local person earned a living by providing various services for 'them', whether doing their laundry, their gardening or other jobs. They had their own social life and private entertainment in their house-parties, dances or balls. The club house on the golf course was only for 'them', but local tradesmen soon formed their own golf club, with offices in nearby premises, and made an arrangement to use the golf course on Thursday afternoons, when the shops were closed, and also on Sunday mornings. If, on account of their excellence, one or other of the members would be invited to play with 'them', they might well refuse, being very conscious of their own dignity. The upper class wives were reputed to be more conscious of their status than their husbands. Mrs so-and-so would not dream of asking a lady of lower social standing to have tea with her. Even children could not associate with anyone they liked and could bring home only those school friends who were of a similar social class. The upper classes would be pleasant and kind to their 'inferiors', but always conscious of their superior status. Also the large houses had a tradesmen's entrance, which was very inconvenient for the delivery of heavy goods as it was always somewhere at the back of the house, a long way from the road.

A few of the large houses, Stoneborough House and Tidwell Barton for example, used to give an annual ball for the sons and daughters of the local tradesmen and farmers. But there was plenty of social life and dancing for everybody in the public rooms and halls, especially during the winter months. There were dance bands made up of local men, whatever their trade, providing they were skilled in playing a musical instrument, and they would often play two or three times a week at local dances in Budleigh Salterton and the nearby villages of East Budleigh, Otterton, Newton Poppleford, Littleham, or sometimes further afield. I should think they must have been very tired at the end of a busy season and often sleepy on the morning following the previous evening's performance.

But life did not consist solely of carnivals and public entertainment. These were the highlights in the days before entertainment was brought into people's houses via radio and television. For the children there was school and for the adults work.

SCHOOL

The school I went to, as did most of the children of the town, was in Queen Street, behind the High Street. We were divided into three sections: the 'infants', the 'big boys' and the 'big girls'. The infants class was mixed; and parents could send their children at the tender age of three – very young for a child to start the then hard life of a schoolchild. The staff consisted of five teachers; one for the infants and four for the two senior departments which had two classrooms each.

The boys' school was heated by a coal- or coke-burning stove, known as a 'Tortoise Stove'. It was a deep tubular affair with a door on the top to pour in the fuel, and another near the bottom for the removal of the ashes. There was a tin filled with water standing on the top, which, as the day wore on, was replenished as required and was, I take it, for the purpose of regulating humidity. The children at the end of the room nearest to it were suffocatingly hot while those at the other end of the room could scarcely get any warmth at all. The youngest class, Standard 1, were at the stove end; the two doors were also at that end and, when opened, caused an icy blast of air through the room. There was a heavy curtain dividing Standard 1 from Standards 4, 5 and 6. Standards 2 and 3 were in a room at the side, divided from the main classroom by sliding doors.

The headmaster, Mr Griffin, was a tyrant, ruling the boys' department very strictly but, I suppose, fairly. He had been the organist at Rolle Chapel. According to the rules of those days the cane was used freely, and protests from parents were ignored. He was a ruler in every sense of the word. If a boy was too late to enter when the door closed at 9 a.m., he was kept waiting outside, winter or summer, until the headmaster was free to attend to the late-comers, usually

School in Queen Street with Mr Griffin the headmaster

95

after prayers, and the punishment was a stripe of the cane on the hand. The boy, so punished, would hardly be able to hold a pen, let alone write, and if there was writing to be done in the next lesson he was then punished for bad handwriting.

The girls' school was upstairs at the other end of the school, which was strictly out of bounds to the boys, and I do not remember ever going up those stairs. But I believe there was a similar layout, and the same strict rules were observed. I never reached the classes taught by Mr Griffin, and after hearing the experiences of those who did, I was always glad.

This state of affairs was revolutionized when, in around 1912, the new St Peter's Church School was built in Moor Lane. A new headmaster named Mullis, a very different kind of teacher, was in charge; he taught the boys' department long after I had left school at the age of thirteen. The classrooms were large and well lit, centrally heated and, for those days, well appointed, with assembly halls in each department, boys' and girls'. I am told that on Monday mornings Mr Mullis used to make a close inspection of the children to see whether they were washed behind the ears and whether their shoes and clothes were clean.

The schools in Queen Street and Moor Lane were sponsored by the Anglican Church and run for the benefit of any local children. Before the turn of the century, parents had to pay one penny a week for each child, which could be quite a burden for the poor if they had several children. A similar school was run at Knowle Village and was attended also by the children from Kersbrook. It too was closed when the new school in Moor Lane opened.

The premises of the old school in Queen Street continued to be used for several years for various classes and activities, such as concerts and entertainment arranged privately, some of them by the Co-op. One was a cookery class for the girls; they had to go to Wilson's Stores on the corner of Chapel Street and buy 1oz. lard or butter, 2oz. sugar, 10oz. flour, 1 egg, etc., to make whatever had been decided by the teacher. Imagine the manager of the store having to weigh out all these small quantities for each of the dozen or so girls!

The reader will remember that in our walk about the town I pointed out quite a number of private schools. They were for every age group and every social class, and came and disappeared according to demand, most of them operating before and during the First World War. There was Miss Carpenter's school in High Street for the boys and girls of local tradesmen; Miss Southcott's school in The Lawn for the daughters of farmers and tradespeople; Miss Long's preparatory school, run on the ground floor of a house in The Square for the sons and daughters of business people. Most of the children moved on to grammar schools in Ottery St Mary, Crediton and Exeter at the age of ten. In 1920 a preparatory school for girls was opened by Miss Tucker in Copplestone Road, and in the 1930s Copplestone House Girls' School at Frewins was started, with Mr Fisher as headmaster. Most of these girls moved on to the Convent School in Exmouth or to High Schools in Exeter. All these were day-schools for local chidren.

In addition there were the boarding schools for the sons and daughters of people not living in the town, many of them colonial officials or army officers. There was Park House Boarding School, with playing-fields in Meadow Close; Otterbourne Boys' School in Coastguard Road (until the house was taken over as a private residence by Lady Mathieson in 1912); Ingleside House Boarding School (until acquired by Colonel Chichester); Montpelier Boarding School for Girls, a famous school at the top of Victoria Place; and finally an Academy for the Sons of Gentlemen, latterly run by Mr Spurway and his daughter Alice at Oak Lodge, a house with extensive grounds along the brook before it reaches Station Road.

THE WAR YEARS

At the outbreak of war in August 1914 I was only a few months past the age of ten, but there are certain things I remember quite well. When the news came through I was on the beach by the bathing machines, and the first thing that came to my mind was that my brother Fred, who was in the 'reserves' would be called up, and what would happen to the business of the bathing machines. I also remember there was a mixed feeling about it all, the fear of what would be happening and also of pride that our country was about to be drawn in

Some Salterton lads off to war. Among them are Tom Burch, Jack Davie, Bob Easton, Walt Marker, Bill Bennet, Len Curtis and Alfred Knowles

Going to join their ships, from left to right, Walt Mears, Tom Sedgemoor, Charlie Mears, Frank Mears, Charlie Pearcey, Jack Pearcey, 'Farmer' Pearcey and Henry Rogers

to fight an enemy aggressor. The feeling of pride was soon dampened as the first casualty lists became known, and the dread of who's family would be next affected the send-off that the different groups had. It seemed as if most of the townsfolk were at the railway station to see them go. Photographs would be taken, sometimes not very flattering to the men in uniform, as they had been celebrating their being called up and were in no fit state to be photographed for such an occasion. The feeling of pride diminished even more as the awful death-roll began to mount, and it was becoming more difficult for the War Office to maintain the fighting forces at the level required. Eventually conscription started, and as men reached the age of eighteen they were called for service and put into one of the fighting forces or into some kind of work to help the war effort. As the war progressed the age was raised and eventually men up to the age of fifty were called before a tribunal, and unless they could produce evidence that the work they were engaged in was of importance to the war effort, they were called up. This led to a system of being given an armband to wear to show that they had been exempted.

There were at the time certain people who considered themselves patriots and would approach anyone they thought should be in the forces and say, 'Where is your armband?', or in some cases give them a white feather, which was the equivalent of calling them a coward. It was embarrassing to some who had not yet been called to the tribunal or, as in the case of one of my brothers, who being six foot tall looked much older than he really was. On being asked on one occasion by a group of young ladies, 'Where is your armband?', he gave them an answer which I will not repeat, but which sent them on their way, more careful of whom they would ask the question in future.

Women were not conscripted, but there was a Women's Army and other groups, including the Land Army. But I remember only two women in Budleigh Salterton who served in the forces in the two world wars, one being my sister Bessie. I myself, as soon as I left school, was pressed to help in the business, as by this time my other brothers, who were of military age, were in the army or navy. Bill served in the Royal Navy in minesweepers, Fred in the Devonshire Regiment, and Frank and Herman in the Royal Marines – a proud record for one family. And luckily all returned safely. My father served in what was known as the Coastal Patrol, formed by the fishermen who were too old for active service, and used to patrol the cliffs in both directions, armed only with a sword-stick, a short walking-stick with a pointed blade inside, and accompanied by a young lad who would have to run back to the Coastguard Station if anything unusual was spotted. Duty was twelve hours on, twelve off. The pay was small, but it was one way for the older men to do their bit for king and country.

Besides conscription there was the requisition of all horses and vehicles that were not essential to the owners to carry on their business. Notice was given that they were to be brought to the Rolle Mews at a stated time and if suitable for the army, would be taken and an agreed price was paid. No horse was allowed to be exempt on personal or sentimental grounds, and there was many a tearful farewell as horses and owners were parted.

The war had not been going long before troops were billeted in the town. The authorities decided how many each household could accommodate, and about four hundred officers and men of the Royal Army Medical Corps arrived in due course, causing great excitement and giving Budleigh Salterton the appearance of a garrison town. The usual activities of men in uniform were watched with great interest, as the various squads of men assembled and marched off to different buildings and parts of the town. One thing I remember was the bugle-calls ringing out at all hours of the day; particular ones being 'Reveille' at about 6.30 a.m., 'Cookhouse', 'Defaulters', which was sounded hourly during the evening, and the 'Last Post' at about 11.00 p.m. The troops stayed, if I remember rightly, for about a year, and the town reverted to normal. Many friendships were formed and not a few romances. The town did not feel the effects of the war a great deal, life went on, more or less, as normal. Of course the men who were away were greatly missed, and when news came of someone who was killed or missing, it seemed that the whole town was shocked.

An incident that I remember well was when a merchant ship was torpedoed off our shore, and one boatload of the crew landed here on the beach. It was a very stormy night, and it was fortunate for them they landed where they did, as another mile or so to the east, they would have landed on rocks under very high cliffs. It was dark and the men were taken in for the night, four of them brought home by my father. I remember that they slept on the floor in front of the kitchen fire as it was a very cold night in the winter. It was hoped that they would have been moved the next day, but they had to spend a second night with us. Somehow – possibly through the generosity of the townspeople, as they had no money of their own – some of them got drunk, and when they came home after closing-time, a Greek, who spoke no English, and an Irishman started a fight. A knife came into sight, and only the quick intervention of my father and one of the other men saved a nasty situation.

On another occasion a British seaplane got into difficulties, landed on the water near the shore and was hauled up the beach by fishermen, using one of the capstans. It remained several days for repairs, then was pushed back into the water and flew off safely. Some time later another plane crash-landed in a field in the Copp Hill area. It was a wreck, but the pilot was not killed, and after treatment, was taken away.

A few war-time restrictions were imposed. One was that you had to apply for a permit to use a boat at sea. Permits were usually issued to cover dawn to dusk, but there must have been exceptions, as the herring-drifters continued fishing and herrings were landed during the war years. Prices were controlled after a few months, and this continued until the end of the war. Rationing of food came later, but not on the scale of the Second World War. It didn't help the poor very much though, for prices rocketed and they couldn't afford to pay for the food that was on their cards. I remember queueing for meat at the butchers' the first time that frozen meat went on sale in the town. It was not very popular, especially on arrival when it was still in its frozen state, and could not be sold until it had thawed. Chocolate and sweets were not rationed but were very hard to get if you didn't know when a shop had received supplies. Within a few days or even hours they would be sold out. Vegetables and fruit were in short supply as the submarine blockade got worse. Quite a lot of fields that had

never been ploughed before came under cultivation, and quite a lot of owners of large gardens had their lawns dug up and planted with vegetables. Even places like Bicton Park came under cultivation and indeed it was considered very unpatriotic not to do so. Things got so bad that people used to pick stringing-nettles to use as cabbage, but not many enjoyed eating them. Economy was a byword and was pressed home almost continually. It was hoped that rhubarb leaves would be a source of food but they proved poisonous. I don't remember any deaths caused by them but they made people violently sick.

As in the Second World War, street-lighting, such as it was then, was severely cut, mostly on the coast, both as an economy and as a protection against the enemy. It was all gas then; the top two-thirds of the large lanterns were painted black and later the remainder white, so that it became very difficult to find your way around. The lamps were lit at dusk, and put out at 10 p.m. by two men employed by the Gas Company. They carried a long pole with a hook and burning taper at the end, which they pushed up through a trap in the bottom of the lantern, thus supplying the necessary air. The gas was turned on and off by means of a tap attached to a bar with a chain at both ends, and a large ring at the end of the chain. By pulling the longer of the chains they lit a small jet of gas called a 'bypass' which in turn ignited the main gas supply. Sometimes, in high wind in exposed positions the gas lamps were blown out and had to be relighted by hand usually by a man with a ladder. However, in the summer months during the long hours of daylight they were not lit at all, and neither were they lit for a few nights at full moon when it was considered unnecessary. The lamp-lighters did their job riding a bicycle. They used to boast that they didn't need to stop, which was perhaps a bit of an exaggeration, but they certainly didn't get off their bikes, and that in itself was quite a feat as the bikes were then very simple machines and not safety models like they are now.

It was part of the Coast Patrol's duty to see that no light was visible from the sea because of the danger from enemy submarines. On most days, mainly in the evening, large convoys of merchant ships would pass the bay, very close to the shore, protected by warships. There were times when it was miraculous that they did not run aground. Entertainment also suffered as it became more and more difficult to see after dark – it was almost a complete black-out. There was quite a number of war songs, as in the Second World War. Among them there were hits like 'It's a long way to Tipperary', 'Dolly Gray' and 'Keep the home fires burning'. They were a great morale-booster as the war dragged on – until, at last, the Armistice was declared. It is difficult to describe the scenes of joy and the feeling of relief that at last peace had come. Everybody that could walk flocked into the streets, laughing, singing, crying and waving flags and banners. Traffic was either halted or made its way around the back streets. Fireworks were let off. Where they came from I couldn't tell as they had been more or less unobtainable since the outbreak of the war. Huge bonfires were lit as darkness came on, often in the middle of the road. One particular one that I remember was in the road outside the Rolle Hotel, where anything that would burn was used. Tar barrels came from nowhere and when well alight were carried around on hurdles. It was a wonder that there were no fires in the many thatched roofs that were still around. The police, assisted by special constables, did all they could to stop it at first, but the crowd were in no mood for interference and eventually the policemen made themselves 'conspicuous by their absence'. This went on well into the night and what a mess was left to be cleared up the next day.

A different kind of mess was to show itself later in the economic depression after the war. There was no social security or automatic unemployment benefit in those days and numbers of ex-servicemen and others without a job were more or less forced to beg to earn a living. They included door-to-door salesmen, who carried in a suitcase small articles such as notepaper, envelopes and small household requirements like brushes, cleaning materials, and also cheap jewellery etc. At times these salesmen were so numerous as to be a nuisance. Street musicians of various talents abounded: from small ex-servicemens' bands to the more common single artists, and brass bands comprised of out-of-work miners from South Wales, who paraded the main streets. I remember two artists who had outstanding qualities and were always welcomed by the patrons of the Bathing Station. One, who later became a programme presenter at the BBCs Bristol studios, could sing in three languages and often did so on his appearances on the beach. He also was invited to sing at the various hotels as an after-dinner attraction. His name was Bernie Edgar and the last time his name appeared on television was when he was presenting the 'Hymns of Praise' programme on Sunday evenings. The other man, whose name I never knew, was a violinist of outstanding talent and, although not as popular as Bernie Edgar, was always welcome and quite popular. I recall these things as a reminder of how our politicians of the day promised that on their return from the war, servicemen would find 'a land fit for heroes to live in', or 'an acre and a cow' for those who were so inclined. But I'm afraid these promises did not materialize. People had to live by their wits or as best they could, in those pre-social security days.

Youth band welcoming home the troops from the First World War

CHARACTERS OF THE OLD TOWN

I think the most colourful character of the old town, must have been William Alford, known to everybody as 'Banjo Alford'. He was a simple man, but helpful to many people, doing various jobs for them. Many amusing stories were told about him, some perhaps true and some, I suspect, were very far-fetched. 'Banjo' had a donkey which had as great a reputation as his master. The story went round that when he took the donkey to the beach to eat the grass on the verge, he put sunglasses on the donkey so that it would eat the pebbles. The end of the donkey happened this way: 'Banjo' had loaded up a small cart and as they were going up a steep incline, the donkey dropped dead, much to 'Banjos' consternation. 'Well I'm blowed', he said, 'the so-and-so has played me many a trick before but this is the first time he's done this to me.'

Another story concerning the donkey involves 'Curly' Sedgemore, who, like many other locals, used to use seaweed as manure for his garden or allotment. 'Curly' had forgotten to ask the local haulier to collect the seaweed from the river mouth area and, of course, if it is left in the sun too long, it shrinks to almost nothing and becomes useless. So that this should not happen, someone suggested that 'Curly' should try and borrow 'Banjo's donkey and cart. It would take several journeys but it would save the seaweed. This he did, and being asked afterwards how he had got on, he said that he would rather have a horse with one leg than ever borrow a donkey again!

Another tale about 'Banjo' must have come about after the donkey had died. Quite often a sympathetic person would ask him to do a job that his simple nature could cope with; in this case it was to deliver a bag of potatoes to a house in East Budleigh, a distance of two miles. He tried to borrow a wheelbarrow for the purpose but, as luck would have it, there was none available and he decided to carry them on his back as he did not want to lose the chance of earning a shilling. So off he went, sack on his back, and when he got to Kersbrook, roughly half-way, he said, 'I'm tired. That'll be far enough today', and carried the potatoes back home. He started off the next morning and, still unable to borrow a wheelbarrow, again carried the potatoes on his back. As he neared the top of Surgery Hill, a gentleman in a car came along and gave him a lift after having enquired where he was going. All cars in those early days of motoring were open tourers. So in got 'Banjo' and away they went. Some time later the gentleman looked and saw 'Banjo' standing up with the sack still on his back. 'Sit down, Alford', he said. 'You'll be more comfortable that way.'

'Oh no', 'Banjo' replied, 'It's very good of you to give me a ride. I'll carry the potatoes.'

Many more stories could be told of his doings, such as the day when he was walking about in the sweltering heat with a heavy overcoat on. The poor chap hadn't got a shirt on that day. Someone suggested to him that, as it was so hot, he would be cooler with the coat off.

'Oh no', he said, 'what keeps out the cold will keep out the heat.'

There were other characters who became as much a part of the old town as the old buildings and streets. Their ways and sayings had been handed down from one generation to the other, and I often find myself doing and saying them especially when talking to people of my age. 'Curly' Sedgemore was a very industrious man if the situation warranted it, and in his later days he owned two or three of the larger boats on the beach, from which he derived a small income. He was the first fisherman to have a boat with a centre keel, a heavy piece of lead allowing the boat to be kept on course against the wind, using sails. One day, as he was collecting crab and lobster pots, the wind freshened to gale force. Instead of running for shelter he carried on until finished, fixed the boat, hoisted the sail and made for the beach. The crabs and lobsters started to crawl overboard and, while he was trying to retrieve them the tiller swung around, the boat capsized, and 'Curly' fell into the water. Fishermen in those days couldn't swim. Indeed, it was considered unlucky for them to be able to do so. 'Curly' managed to hang on to the boat and was saved by another fisherman who heard his cries for help. But boat and catch went down, a serious loss to him. Mr Russell, manager of Lloyds' Bank in Fore Street, came to his rescue by organizing a subscription, and out of gratitude 'Curly' and his wife Jemima, called their son, who was born to them some two years later, Russell

Sedgemore. I never saw 'Curly' enter a public house but he didn't die a rich man. He was always respected and always willing to help others in any way he could.

There were also two brothers Mark and Kip Matthews, two quite different types of men. Mark was very fond of cider. He used to go from his house in lower Granary Lane to the local pub in the High Street and buy two, or more, of the flat bottles, holding a quart each of draught cider, put them in a sack across his shoulders and carry them home; you could hear the bottles rattling as he walked. On reaching the public toilets on the Parade his thirst would always be greater than he could bear and he would go inside and take a good swig. Kip was a small man, always dressed as a typical navvy, and worked on any project that was going, usually for Palmers, who contracted for most work. A strict rule of the firm was no smoking during working hours. Kip was once working on a pipe-laying track, digging a trench, in those days with a pick and shovel. In this case Kip was working for another firm, J. Pantoll, who allowed smoking during work time. Mr Palmer, being in the area where Pantoll's men were working, took a look in the trench and, seeing Kip smoking away like a chimney, said to him,' I see you can do two things at once, Matthews', meaning that he was smoking while he was at work. Kip, who never minced his words replied, 'Yes, Mr Palmer, I can do three things at once.' 'Oh, said Mr Palmer, 'how can you do that?' Quick as a flash came the reply, 'I can work, smoke and mind my own bloody business. Good Day Mr Palmer'.

Then there was Jim Pidgeon, who used to walk very slowly; if one greeted him one would get a reply a few steps away. Anyone who didn't know him might have taken Jim for a surly old man, but in fact, he was a nice old boy. Another one was Jack Heard, he was very tall, and very lean with it. It was a local joke that Palmers always employed him to paint the inside of the rainwater down-pipes. He was reputed to have a brother who, Jack said, was so like him that they could not be recognized apart, the only difference being that his brother was a little bit taller 'but hardly so big about'.

Most of these characters were natives of the town or its surroundings. But there was one man, 'Uncle John', a member of the Gardener Wholesale Grocery Firm of Bristol. The Gardener family had visited Budleigh Salterton for a number of years during the more prosperous times of the company. 'Uncle John' was very eccentric but a lovable character, and could get away with almost anything. On the occasion of the Prince of Wales' visit to Bicton House, one of the Prince's official duties was to inspect the local branch of the British Legion, formerly known as the 'Comrades of the Great War'. Walking along the line of ex-soldiers, he was shaking hands with each one, and as he came to the end of the line, 'Uncle John' stepped forward and received the royal handshake – and was very proud of it! He had no family of his own, and in his later years bought 'East Cliff' on Marine Parade. It was then still a three-storey house, and he could ill afford to run it alone. He tried his hand at many things, including making and bottling an ink of his own brand, which bore the name 'Jetta' and the inscription, 'When writing a letter, we want you to think, how much better is Jetta, and costs the same chink'. But it was, like most of his later ventures, a failure. His last enterprise was dealing in secondhand furniture and bric-a-brac, and for this he rented the old barn in Barn Lane, near the railway arch. I bought a very delicate tea set from him, either Japanese or Chinese, so very delicate to be almost weightless, and every piece has a different pattern. I like to think it may be valuable, but I shall keep it, if only to remind me of 'Uncle John'!

CHANGE AND PROGRESS

The biggest change affecting people's lives must surely have been the coming of the motor car. In 1912 there were five privately-owned cars in Budleigh Salterton. The owners were Mr Hughes of Cintra, Dr Semple of Abele Tree House, Colonel Chichester of Ingleside House, Mrs Fulton of Dial House and Mr and Mrs Keep who lived at Fountain Hill. As they were unable to drive the cars, they had to have a chauffer, who was very often also the gardener. For everyone else transport was by horse-drawn vehicles. These varied, according to requirement. For a day out you could hire a carriage drawn by two horses. It would carry up to six passengers, seated facing each other. For larger parties, of eight or ten, there was a vehicle called a brake,

Mariah Gibbon's donkey cart in Moor Lane

which was drawn by four horses. For shorter journeys around the town there were the smaller carriages, from open landaus to – for those days – very posh broughams, which were completely enclosed against the weather and beautifully appointed inside. There was also a pony phaeton, and a pony bath-chair (which was very much in demand by invalids), or a pony and trap. The drivers were very skilled at their job and would go to any length to see that their patrons were well looked after. They also took great pride in their personal appearance, as well as that of their horses, the harnesses and carriages. And just as there are now garages for emergencies, in those days there would be stabling where, usually with the help of a local blacksmith, repairs could be carried out.

For longer journeys there was the railway, to which Budleigh Salterton was linked up in 1903. It was also the chief means of transporting all types of goods, including coal. Goods were taken from the station by horse and wagon to shops and other destinations. There was also a goods service between Budleigh Salterton and Exeter,

Mrs Jack Cowd in a bath-chair-like donkey cart

via East Budleigh and other villages en route, operated by Mr Frank Watts. He had a wagon drawn by two shire horses and made the journey three times a week; outwards on Mondays, Wednesdays and Fridays and homewards on the following days. The journey would take all day and the wagon often did not get back until very late. Frank Watts eventually replaced the old horse-drawn service with a steam wagon, a Foden, which speeded things up a bit. A daily service was now possible but this too gave way to progress. A motor truck was used next, driven by Frank's son Eddie, and the Foden, together with its driver, became obsolete.

Very soon after the First World War there was a passenger service between Exeter and Budleigh Salterton, operated by the Devon General Bus Company; it offered a very crude and uncomfortable ride! The vehicle was a converted army lorry with seating installed but open to the weather at the sides. Later, Mr Percy Hart started another service between Exmouth and Ladram Bay. Competition between the two was very fierce, resulting in the fares being drastically reduced; at one time to sevenpence return to Exmouth. In the town itself there was a station bus which used to meet all the trains and take passengers to any destination for sixpence, luggage included, but relying on tips to make up the driver's meagre wage. What would now be regarded as a taxi service was run as a business by several operators, including the Rolle Mews, the Feathers Hotel, and a Mr Tom Fayter, in Chapel Street, who also had a shoe-repairing business.

One of the effects of the greater mobility of the public after the First World War was a booming tourist industry in the town. Large private family houses, too big for their owners to keep up without several servants, were turned into elegant hotels. They included Otterbourne House, Ingleside House and Blueberry Downs (formerly Ottermouth House). At the same time the once flourishing business of private education seemed to be on the decline, and the houses that had served as boarding schools, for example Montpelier and Park House, were also used for visitors to the town. The existing hotels, such as

Frank Watts taking delivery of a new Foden. From left to right, the driver who brought it from the North of England (two-days' journey), Frank Watts with his daughter, and Tommy Yeoman, his driver

First passenger service, a converted army lorry with seating installed, but open to the weather on the sides

Hart's Bus operating between Exmouth and Ladram Bay (1927)

Methodist Choir outing in a charabanc. Mr Arundell, choirmaster and organist is in the centre of the picture

the Rosemullion and the Rolle, built extensions and annexes at intervals, not always enhancing the beautiful architecture of the original house! So great was the demand for accommodation that these and other hotels hired every available room in private houses in the High Street and other nearby roads. People took great care in their dress, and if you wanted to dine at the Rosemullion, for instance, the ladies had to wear long gowns and the gentlemen, dress suits with tails. You could see a fashion show or spectacle, free of charge, when the guests made their way from their various lodgings to the hotel in the evening.

At one time there were seven hundred bedrooms available for holiday makers in the town. The boom was not limited to hotels only, private houses had their share in it. The reader will have noticed the frequent references to apartment or boarding houses in our 'walk about the town'. Apartment houses were private houses lived in by a family, with the husband pursuing his trade, while the wife let rooms to visitors who bought their own food, which she cooked and served to them in the hired rooms. Boarding houses had a similar arrangement, except that people did not provide their own food but had it served to them, much as in a present-day guest house. It even happened that owners of suitable houses let their own homes to visitors for the summer while they themselves went off to live in France, where life was cheaper at that time.

During the Second World War large numbers of military people were billeted in this holiday accommodation, and after the war tourism gradually faded away. Many of the larger houses have disappeared and been replaced by modern blocks of flats. Those that still exist have either been converted into flats or been adapted for the care of elderly people. Many of the families who occupied them have gone also, either leaving the town or, in many instances, forced to live in smaller properties to enable them to carry on. But great as the change has been for these families, the change in the standard of living of the working classes must have been still greater. Young couples getting married today start off

Increased mobility brings 'trippers' to the Parade — a taste of things to come

A last look at Budleigh Salterton in the 1920s, before the drastic changes took place

with most of the things that their grandparents could never even have hoped to acquire after many years of marriage. Holidays with pay, except for the very few, were unheard of. Bank Holidays could be taken, but pay was deducted. And as working hours were much longer there was little spare time for other activities. Wages were low, and as there were so many large families, little money was available for things that in these times are taken for granted. Some speak of 'the good old days'; but having experienced both the old and the new, I know which I prefer! And yet Budleigh Salterton, the town in which I grew up, and Poplar Row as it was then, simple cottages with none of the modern luxuries, will ever be dear to me.